from Susan

? Xmas 2015

WRINKLIES'™ HOLIDAY PUZZLES

THIS IS A CARLTON BOOK

Published in 2012 by Prion
An imprint of the Carlton Publishing Group
20 Mortimer Street
London W1T 3JW

Layout and design copyright © 2012 Carlton Books Limited
Wrinklies is a trademark of Carlton Books Ltd

This book is sold subject to the condition that it shall not, by way of trade
or otherwise, be lent, resold, hired out or otherwise circulated without the
publisher's prior written consent in any form of cover or binding other than
that which it is published and without a similar condition, including this
condition, being imposed upon the subsequent purchaser. All rights reserved

A CIP catalogue record of this book can be obtained from the British
Library

ISBN 978 1 85375 850 8

Printed and bound by CPI Group (UK) Ltd, Croydon, CR0 4YY

10 9 8 7 6 5 4 3 2 1

The puzzles in this book previously appeared in *Brain Training Puzzles:
Quick Book 1, Quick Book 2, Intermediate Book 1, Intermediate Book 2,
Difficult Book 1, Difficult Book 2, House of Puzzles Holiday Puzzles, House
of Puzzles Travel Puzzles, House of Puzzles Sudoku, Lateral Thinking
Puzzles, Lateral Thinking Posers*

WRINKLIES'™ HOLIDAY PUZZLES

Conundrums for older intellects

CARLTON

Contents

Introduction

The key to staying youthful is keeping the mind active. In your senior years you (hopefully) have more time to devote to hobbies and pastimes, and there is no better way to pass the time than giving your grey matter a workout.

Puzzles are particularly useful in sharpening your perception, memory, logic and reasoning – all of which can become casualties in your autumn years if you chose to stimulate your brain with nothing more thought provoking than the TV guide.

The conundrums in this book have been specially chosen with the Wrinkly puzzle-lover in mind. We hope you enjoy this collection and remember that where the mind goes, the heart will follow. Here's to many more years of youth.

EASY
PUZZLES

Word search

```
D K T H A M E S E G S R X K E
R R B I B L E L R C O D E X D
A A G G A R D E N B U S M W Y
U P B Q A E E W W A T A E M H
G L O B E N S E O N H S A A T
E S S N E T G J R K T D A H E
C F M H O Y A O C M A I L G G
G R T N E V O C I M J C B N D
N A E J J Z L N E B E K E I I
I H T G A V S G O I C E R K R
G J O T N T M E L G I N T C B
N G V J E I A A L B L S J U L
A E Y R E S G T G E A E Z B E
H J N O D N O L E N S X N Y M
C A U D G P A R L I A M E N T
```

ABBEY	ELGIN	LONDON
ALBERT	EYE	MADAME
ALICE	EYRE	MAGNA
BANK	GAOL	NEEDLE
BIBLE	GARDEN	PARK
BIG BEN	GINGER	PARLIAMENT
BRIDGE	GLOBE	ROSETTA
BUCKINGHAM	GREEN	SOUTH
CHANGING	GUARD	STONE
CODEX	HYDE	TATE
COVENT	JANE	THAMES
CROWN	JEWELS	WESTMINSTER
DICKENS	JOHN	ZOO

Spot the difference

Can you spot ten differences between this pair of pictures?

5				7				3
4	3	7				2	6	1
1				4				7
	4			9			2	
9		3	7	8	2	4		6
			9		8			
3	1			6			5	9
			5		1			

Tents and trees

Every tree ▲ has one tent △ found horizontally or vertically adjacent to it. No tent can be in an adjacent square to another tent (even diagonally!). The numbers by each row and column tell you how many tents are there. Can you locate all the tents?

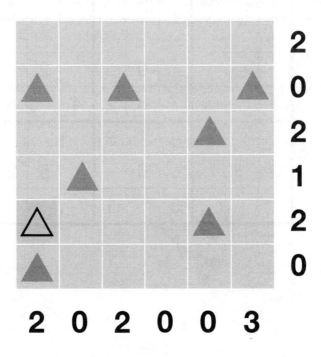

The slow horses

Alexander, the aged and eccentric king of Draconia, decided to abdicate but could not make up his mind which of his two sons should sit on his throne. He finally decided that, as his sons were both accomplished horsemen, he would hold a race in which the loser, i.e. the owner of the slowest, rather than the fastest horse, would become king.

Each of the sons owned a superb horse and feared that the other would cheat by holding his own horse back, so they agreed to consult the wisest man in the kingdom. With only two words, the wise man ensured that the race would be fair. What did he say?

Sudoku

3					7			
		6			1			
	1	2	6	4				
		5				4		3
		1		9	3			6
7	9			6	8			
			7			8	2	4
						6		
			8	3		5		7

Spot the difference

Can you spot ten differences between this pair of pictures?

```
T D Y T O P O T T E M L E H Y
E M A G R D L E I F N I O E S
K B N O T U O N R H F O K F O
C E P E C Z N S O N P C Y W C
I R S S E T J L N B O L O S C
R P E A V R E V O H U R X P E
C U L K B I G O L F H L I M R
S C S L N W O O D T F N C U B
S K V O B U Y F Y T G E T T O
H T N V K L B Y A P R E N S W
C E R E L R A W O I E A N S L
T M A I D E N N P T R U V L E
A A S V K U G M U C C W A E R
M D E Y U E U Z U H W B A T L
P Z L K J T R O G Q M O S Y A
```

BALL	HOLE-IN-ONE	PROP
BASE	HOOP	PUCK
BAT	INFIELD	RUN
BOWLER	IRON	SET
BUNKER	LOVE	SILLY
CLUB	MAIDEN	SOCCER
CRICKET	MATCH	STRIKER
FAIRWAY	NET	STUMPS
GAME	OFFENSE	TEE
GOLF	OUT	THROW
GREEN	OVER	TRAVEL
HELMET	PING PONG	UMPIRE
HOCKEY	PITCH	WOOD

Spot the difference

Can you spot ten differences between this pair of pictures?

Tents and trees

Every tree ▲ has one tent △ found horizontally or vertically adjacent to it. No tent can be in an adjacent square to another tent (even diagonally!). The numbers by each row and column tell you how many tents are there. Can you locate all the tents?

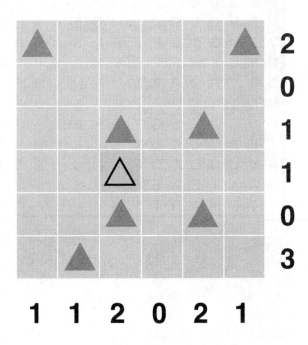

Word search

```
K S T E W N C G E C I U J C L
D E G E O N M U J P S L U T I
I G B N M C A H P A C R P U I
S C G A N I H E L F R L F C K
H I X O B T L A S Y U S L K Q
M E V O L C D G R G B L A E V
V E H G I B P O K M B A N R U
N M U F A F F B E K I V K Y A
U R V R D R A L U K N I S E I
M A I N E R T E E A G A B Y R
F S O A P S G T G R B N S P G
T E A C L C U V G L R L B U N
K M U G O C O F E N U A E B A
C W A I E A E R N I S M G M S
J T U M A R T I N I H J Z A Y
```

BAKER	FLANK	OVEN
BEAUNE	GOBLET	PLUG
BUN	HAM	SABLE
CAN	INFUSER	SAGE
CHAR	JUICE	SALAD BAR
CLOVE	KEBAB	SALT BOX
COAT	LARD	SANGRIA
CORN	LIME	SCRUBBING BRUSH
CUPFUL	MARTINI	SINK
CURRY	MELBA	SOAP
DISH	MELTS	STEW
ECLAIR	MIGNON	TUCKER
EGGS	MUG	VEAL

Sudoku

2		7		1			4	
		8						2
			9			5	1	
4		1	2	5		3		
3				4				1
		5		3	1	9		4
	3	2			6			
8						4		
	9			8		2		3

Changing the odds

In a distant kingdom lived a king who had a beautiful daughter. She fell in love with a humble peasant boy whom she wanted to marry. The king, who had no intention of consenting to the marriage, suggested instead that the decision be left to chance. The three were standing in the castle's forecourt, which was covered with innumerable white and black pebbles. The king claimed to have picked up one of each colour and put the two pebbles into his hat. The suitor had to remove one pebble from the hat. A white pebble meant that he could marry the king's daughter; a black, that he was never to see her again.

The peasant boy was poor but not stupid. He noticed that by sleight of hand the king had put two black pebbles into the hat. How did the suitor resolve his predicament without calling the king a cheat?

Sudoku

3		1			9			
					6		3	
7	8	6	3	5				
	3					9	4	
	1		4	3	5		7	
	6	4					5	
				4	3	7	1	9
	5		6					
			1			5		8

Spot the difference

Can you spot ten differences between this pair of pictures?

Sudoku

	7							9
5	8		1					3
		3		8			5	
			2		3	4		5
		1			8			6
			4		6	7		1
		4		5			3	
3	9		8					7
	5							8

Insomnia

IBM executives held a sales conference at a hotel in Miami. Pete and Dave occupied rooms overlooking the swimming pool. After a strenuous day of presentations and partying, they went to their rooms. Despite being exhausted, Pete just could not get off to sleep. Eventually, at about two in the morning, he called the switchboard and asked to be put through to Dave's room. As soon as Dave picked up the phone, Pete replaced his and fell asleep.

Explain.

9		1			2			
7			9	1	8	5		
		3				1		
			4				1	5
2	5			8			6	9
1	7				6			
		5				3		
		6	8	3	5			1
			6			9		8

Every tree ▲ has one tent △ found horizontally or vertically adjacent to it. No tent can be in an adjacent square to another tent (even diagonally!). The numbers by each row and column tell you how many tents are there. Can you locate all the tents?

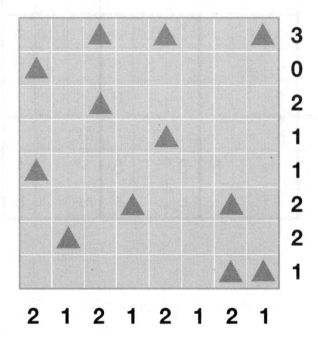

Sudoku

2							9	
5			6		7	1		
	3	1						7
	1		2	6				4
	2		1	8	5		7	
9				7	3		2	
8						2	1	
		5	3		8			9
	9							3

Sudoku

			9	7	3			
	2					3		5
			1				8	
		2					6	
					7			1
	9	6	4			8		
	5		6	1				
		1	7			2		3
	8	4						

```
R Y O R K H C I W R O N S B S
A M E W B N L L U H S W F R N
M D A Y R Y O U G M R O F L O
S S F C E Y V I T U E T O B D
R R B O C Y R U B O G C T Y L
O E T M H A A V S L N B O R O
K G T B I B M O L I A O W L S
M I A E N L E S L C R A O U S
W T I L X U K T U L I C T N J
C C R E W E O Y G Y A T I A D
E F O R E S T X T B O B Y H E
L S T N I A S H N N O S I T T
T W H T U O M E N R U O B I I
I C D V D R O F T A W O O A N
C L Y D E A O L D H A M C R U
```

ALBION	EXETER	RANGERS
ALLOA	FOREST	REDS
BLUES	GULLS	ROBINS
BORO	HULL	SAINTS
BOURNEMOUTH	JAYS	STOKE
BRECHIN	LINCOLN	SUTTON
BURY	LUTON	TIGERS
CELTIC	MACCAMS	TOFFS
CITY	NORWICH	TOWN
CLYDE	OLDHAM	UNITED
COUNTY	OWLS	WATFORD
CREWE	RAITH	WYCOMBE
DONS	RAMS	YORK

Spot the difference

Can you spot ten differences between this pair of pictures?

3				2			5	
7		2			8		6	
		6	7		1			
8	4						9	
	1		5	4	2		3	
	2						7	4
			3		4	2		
	3		2			6		7
	6			9				5

Accident prone

Steve Jones, an architect, was inspecting his latest project, a brownstone conversion in the upper east side of Manhattan. He was very proud of the finished building and was inspecting the roof when he slipped and fell over the edge to the concrete forecourt below, landing catlike on all fours. Surprisingly he escaped with only heavy bruising and shock.

A week later he was feeling fit enough to return to the building, and again finished up on the roof. In a stroke of amazing bad luck and in an almost complete replay of the previous week's events, he tripped and fell, again landing on all fours in the same spot on the concrete forecourt. This time, however, he broke both legs and arms, and was hospitalized for several weeks.

The amazing thing was that during his fall he realized that, for a reason beyond his control, on this occasion he would be badly injured. How did he know?

							1	5
	4			8				
2	6		1			8		4
8		1			4			
9			8	2	3			1
5		6			7			
6	5		2			9		8
	8			3				
							6	3

Crossword

Across

6. Space voyager (9)
7. Our star (3)
8. Spicy (3)
9. Floor washer (3)
11. Confused (5-2)
13. Airborne forces (3)
14. Rent out (3)
16. Beer (3)
17. Frozen deluge (9)

Down

1. Haberdasher's goods (8)
2. Post (4)
3. Score (4)
4. Customary (6)
5. Preparation (4-2)
10. Solitaire (8)
11. Sweet quick-bread (6)
12. Wood sugar (6)
15. Acquired (4)
16. Charitable donations (4)

Only two of these pictures are exactly the same. Can you spot the matching pair?

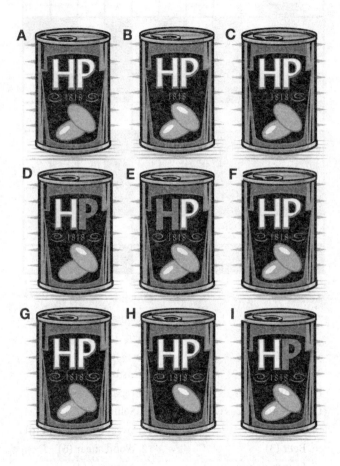

Spot the difference

Can you spot ten differences between this pair of pictures?

```
H J C D C Y C L O P S I R O D
D T J S T A J E S A P Q N N J
P A E F I R D S U E H P R O Y
S R I S T D Q A E K I C E H Y
A U O A A Y T R P K N P B P S
T L S T N H I G Y H X M R O N
O I G A E S B U Z E N A R R T
A E A N G U S S W O H E M E Y
R H E R M E S Z R Y D N A L P
T T A L C E P A N S H A I L H
E E G A E H H I S O E D R E O
M L R O H C I N T A S X P B N
I G P Y M Y T A Y H T A N X B
S M E P A S D R X C I P J B U
S A L L A P Q U A F A I A G B
```

ARES	GAEA	NAIAD
ARGUS	GAIA	ORPHEUS
ARTEMIS	GE	PALLAS
ATHENE	GRACES	PEGASUS
BELLEROPHON	HARPY	PRIAM
CHAOS	HERMES	PROTEUS
CHARON	HESTIA	PSYCHE
CYCLOPS	HYDRA	SOL
DAPHNE	ICHOR	SPHINX
DORIS	IO	STYX
ELECTRA	JASON	TITAN
ERIS	LETHE	TYPHON
EROS	MAENAD	URANIA

Shape shifting

Fill in the empty squares so that each row, column and long diagonal contains five different symbols

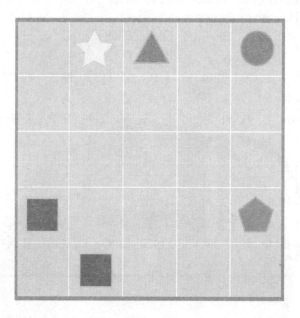

Riddle

In my shed at home I have some hamsters and some hamster cages. If I put one hamster in each cage I'd have one hamster too many. But if I put two hamsters in each cage, I'd have one cage left over... How many hamsters and cages have I got?

Maze

Word search

```
A O S X M E L O T R O N J E M
V S N M B I N K P B A B F U T
I Y O A V N R G O G H I R C E
R O Y N I A O E R L F D E H N
G M A D D P H O L S L R B A O
I S H A W M P T G G U E E N R
N L C K W I L G A O U A C G S
A N Y C I T A R B B N B E P A
L L Q R J L L M T K O G A N X
L B A Q E N A G A E D R I L O
N L A B U T B G P R T V J O P
H I E N M A U O E M I L T I H
A U B B J Y I L N R G M P V O
R U H P H O C L F E E E B P N
P J X X S E M I H C S B V A E
```

ALPHORN	DRUM	QUAIL
ANVIL	FIFE	REBEC
BANJO	FLUTE	REGAL
BELL	GONG	SHAWM
BIN	HARP	TABOR
BONES	LYRE	TAMBOUR
BUGLE	MARIMBA	TENOR SAXOPHONE
CELLO	MELOTRON	TIMPANI
CHANG	MOOG	TRAPS
CHIMES	OBOE	TUBA
CITAR	ORGAN	VINA
CYMBAL	PIANO	VIOL
DEAGAN	PIPE	VIRGINAL

Spot the difference

Can you spot ten differences between this pair of pictures?

More or less

The arrows indicate whether a number in a box is greater or smaller than an adjacent number. Complete the grid so that all rows and columns contain the numbers 1 to 5.

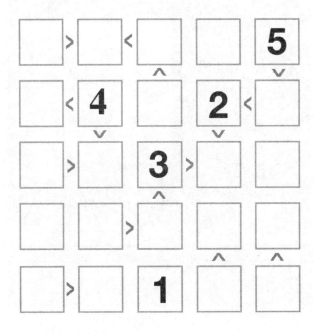

Pots of dots

How many dots should there be in the hole in this pattern?

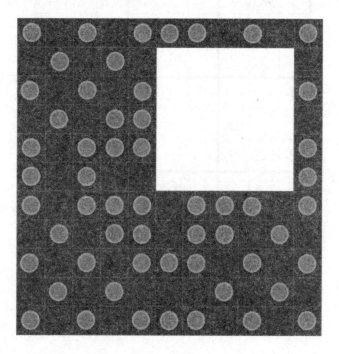

	7				3			4
							2	
		3		5				8
4			5					7
		5	2	9	6	3		
2			7					9
		1		6				5
							9	
	5				7			2

Word search

```
T W W U S T A R B O A R D Z M
A W F O R E C A S T L E U O R
C P S A L P R E C I F F O V E
K E G A R E E T S R N R M E S
L E N N U G B E A T E P E R R
E C P I H S G M W T I D S H U
B R I D G E E N A I R V S E P
B O B Y T S A T A A N N A A P
M W R E H Z S Q O G T G K D O
A S L L W R Y B R S K S S H R
E N L L A Z A O S E T C I E T
B E A A R N B W G T D A A L R
A S F G T O P S I D E D C L O
S T E W A R D V Y F C R A K B
R M H T B U L W A R K A N L X
```

ABOARD	FALL	SHIP
AFT	FORECASTLE	SOS
BEAM	FRAMES	STACK
BELOW	GALLEY	STARBOARD
BLACK GANG	GUNNEL	STATEROOM
BOAT	LADDER	STEERAGE
BOW	LIST	STERN
BRIDGE	MESS	STEWARD
BULWARK	OFFICER	TACKLE
CROW'S NEST	OVERHEAD	THWART
DAVITS	PORT	TOPSIDE
DECK	PURSER	WINGS

Where's the pair?

Only two of these pictures are exactly the same. Can you spot the matching pair?

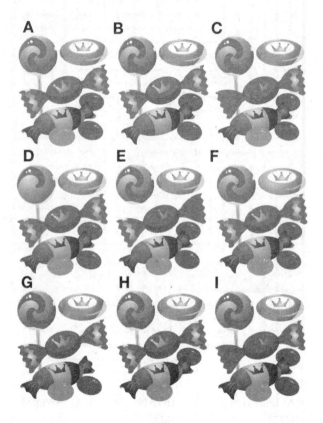

Word search

```
C D A S E R I A S O N E U B Q
F O I W M E X I C A N M S H J
B Z P U O Z N A C C R A E L H
N E A K L I B Y A N U L U I U
A A L B A N Y L T R E T L S N
M I D T H S I R I N O A E B A
R D A N W F A G A M M M S O N
E N D L O A S M E L A S E N Q
G I I R F T Y O O R C O N G O
Z A N G P B S B I A I R A N V
L I I E H K D U A H N A P B V
A A R U B A S A O N O C A V G
P U T T U U Z M H H D I J Y K
E A F A T M A O L C B I M U P
N P B H L N A W A T T O T R D
```

ACCRA	HOUSTON	NEPAL
ALBANY	HUNAN	NIGERIA
APIA	ICAROS	OHIO
ARUBAS	INDIA	OMAN
BELTWAY BANDIT	IOWA	OTTAWAN
BHUTAN	IRISH	PERU
BUENOS AIRES	JAPANESE	ROME
CALIFORNIA	LIBYAN	SALEM
CHAD	LIMA	SAMOAN
CONGO	LISBON	TRINIDAD
DC	MALI	UK
GERMAN	MALTA	USA
HELENA	MEXICAN	UTAH

Spot the difference

Can you spot ten differences between this pair of pictures?

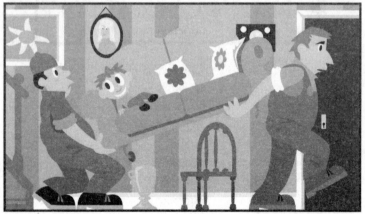

Word search

```
H X G I E K C E O G E N T G A
M C B T O R A N G E F O B W U
C R A B A P P L E A O L I V E
O D R E N N E T F I G L T X L
X K B T P I G N U T Q E T Q K
D H A P R Z A E W E P R E U N
W E D K S U A A L P A O R E U
H P O P I A H P A O P M A E T
O Y S K E G R W O X I R L N K
R D C E P C P R J T N G M I Z
T U H G M A A I X O E R O N R
W R E R W I Z N T M G O N G H
J I R I P A L T T R B U D G K
V A R O I V R U S S E T U B K
J N Y T H U N G C O L M A R S
```

ARNOT	GROUT	PECAN
BARBADOS CHERRY	HAW	PIGNUT
BITTER ALMOND	HEP	QUEENING
COLMAR	HIP	RASP
COX	KAKI	RENNET
CRAB-APPLE	LIME	RUSSET
DATE	MORELLO	SKEG
DURIAN	NUTMEG	TANGELO
EGRIOT	OGEN	UGH
ELK NUT	OLIVE	UVA
FIG	ORANGE	WHORT
GAGE	PAWPAW	WHURT
GENIPAP	PEACH	ZAPOTE

Can you spot ten differences between this pair of pictures?

	3		5	9	1		2	
2								1
	9		2	4	8		7	
	6						1	
3			9		6			7
9				2				8
1		9				2		3
				6				
		5				7		

X and O

The numbers around the edge of the grid describe the number of X's in the vertical, horizontal and diagonal lines connecting with that square. Complete the grid so that there is an X or O in every square.

1	3	3	4	5	1
4				X	3
2	O				4
3			O		3
4					3
1	1	4	3	3	1

1	6			9		8	5	
8	4	5			1			3
		3		5		1		
6		8						
			3				6	7
2		4						
		6		3		2		
3	2	7			8			5
4	1			2		6	3	

Figure it out

The sequence 6789 can be found once in the grid, reading up, down, backwards, forwards or diagonally. Can you pick it out?

7	6	8	7	6	8	9	8	9	9	8	8
8	7	7	6	7	7	6	6	6	6	6	6
8	8	7	8	8	9	8	9	8	8	9	9
9	7	7	8	8	8	9	7	9	7	8	8
6	6	8	6	7	7	7	8	7	9	7	7
8	9	8	7	8	9	8	9	8	8	7	9
9	8	7	8	9	8	9	6	6	9	8	6
7	8	9	7	6	6	6	8	9	6	6	8
8	6	8	9	8	9	8	9	8	8	9	9
9	9	6	6	9	8	9	8	7	6	7	7
6	7	9	8	6	6	7	8	7	9	8	8
8	9	7	9	8	9	8	9	6	8	9	6

		6		7		4		
4	9						6	8
			4		1			
		7	9	1	2	3		
6								9
			3		6			
	6						4	
9								1
	1			5			2	

The galaxy

The First National Museum in midtown Manhattan opened the autumn season with a special attraction – the world's third-largest emerald, called the "Galaxy", worth a king's ransom. The stone was placed in the centre room of the west wing with the tightest security the museum had ever seen.

Touching the crystal glass dome protecting the stone triggered audio and optical alarms. Steel shutters would lock all exits within four seconds. The showcase was supervised by closed-circuit television. In other words, robbery was unthinkable.

On opening day, visitors had to line up and were only admitted in groups of 45. Among the second group allowed in, one character caused considerable annoyance. He was obviously the worse for drink, staggering from room to room, always lagging behind the others.

The group had just left the centre room when all alarms went off. Within five seconds the security guards and a police officer arrived at the scene. The crystal glass dome was shattered and the man was lying on the floor in a drunken stupor. In his left hand he held the Galaxy.

The whisky flask in his right hand was empty. At the prison hospital, he was found to have an alcohol level five times over the limit. In due course he was given a two-year suspended sentence for wilful damage and disorderly conduct. When he left the courtroom, he was an extremely happy and richer man. Why?

Word search

```
M Q H U T P H H E S T O N P M
O A P A U N D A U J H O O U C
M O E C R R E T Y F Y D T R C
N N D H A L T R G E O F G L A
J I T Y C O I O B O S R N E M
S V T C N T P N W K G I I Y B
T O I E Z S P H G E R E D E E
N T D U N E T B C T R R D L R
Y C Y R N R D N N R O N A B W
E H M G O O A O O F O N P M E
L E E N Z F D B L T Q Y O E L
X L R J T N Y I C D R R D W L
E S I N E D M A C U D E W O S
B E T H N A L G R E E N M R N
J A H A R R O W N C O O M B E
```

ACTON	CROYDON	MERTON
BARNET	DRAYTON	MORDEN
BETHNAL GREEN	ERITH	NORTHWOOD
BEXLEY	FOREST	PADDINGTON
BRENT	FRIERN	PENGE
CAMBERWELL	HAM	PURLEY
CAMDEN	HARLINGTON	SIDCUP
CHEAM	HARROW	SUTTON
CHELSEA	HAYES	TOWER
CITY	HENDON	UPON
COOMBE	HESTON	WEMBLEY
CRAYFORD	ILFORD	

MEDIUM
PUZZLES

Word grid

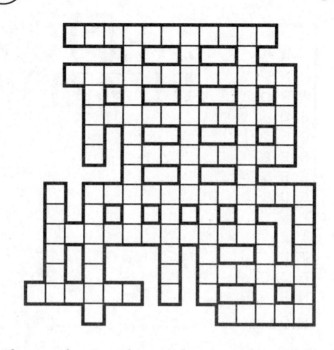

5 letter words
ENDUE
ROUSE
SMELL
STEAK

6 letter words
BODICE
GIGOLO
LATELY
LIB-DEM
SALAMI

7 letter words
LANGUID
RUN AMOK

9 letter words
EFFECTUAL
SWEETPEAS

11 letter words
GO UP IN SMOKE
KUALA LUMPUR
PROOFREADER
UNFORTUNATE

12 letter words
ARMOURED
CARS
GENERAL STORE
LADY'S SLIPPER

```
S P R O U T S R A D I S H N S
E N B E L Y O N Y C S L E E K
D N E O K R A R F E N N E L O
W R O E T A Z M R W O R R A M
S O A N R A I C L A O Y K D O
O C D T O G M S E T C A R I P
B E A N S I E O N K L U S E Z
E B N L C U N E T E O A A S Q
E D D B L O M O I G G O Q F T
L S E S L I L Y L E T Y I I U
T E L W P M O E Z A R T C N R
T U I U S A M N T E C H N G N
E J O Z P I P O L H I Y C E I
N B N F B Z P E T L O K O R P
C H I V E E C H I C O R Y S K
```

BEAN	GOURD	PEA
BEET	GREENS	PIMENTO
CARROT	KALE	POTATO
CELERY	LADIES' FINGERS	PULSE
CHICORY	LEEK	RADISH
CHILI	LENTIL	SAGE
CHIVE	MAIZE	SCALLION
COLE	MARROW	SOY
CORN	MUSTARD	SPROUTS
CRESS	NETTLE	SWEDE
DANDELION	OKRA	TOMATO
FENNEL	ONION	TURNIP
FITCH		YAM

Across

7. Ceramics (11)
8. Sneaker (7)
10. Setting (5)
12. Precise (5)
13. Breather (7)
17. Control (5-6)

Down

1. Warm (4)
2. Diversify (7)
3. Mongolian ruler (4)
4. Starter (6)
5. Auto (3)
6. Holiday destination (6)
9. Flat (7)
10. Split (6)
11. Job (6)
14. Lather (4)
15. Of all time (4)
16. Adipose (3)

Spot the difference

Can you spot ten differences between this pair of pictures?

Maze

Tents and trees

Every tree ▲ has one tent △ found horizontally or vertically adjacent to it. No tent can be in an adjacent square to another tent (even diagonally). The numbers by each row and column tell you how many tents are there. Can you locate all the tents?

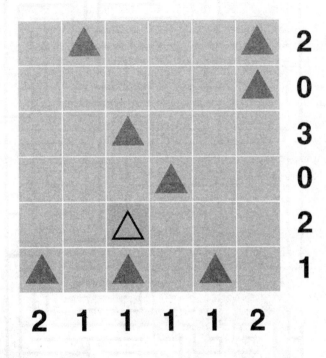

The birthday

Alice and George were window shopping in London's Bond Street. As they passed a jeweller, Alice stopped and admired a bracelet, one of three, with the motif of a leopard silhouetted in semi-precious stones. Reading her mind, her husband said, "Darling, I would love to make this your birthday present, but it must be far beyond my budget." "Let's ask, just for fun," ventured Alice, and they entered the store. As requested, the sales clerk fetched the leopard bracelet. Alice tried it on and looked pleadingly at her husband. Asked the price, the clerk hesitated for a brief moment and then said, "£250 for payment in cash." George could not hide his surprise, as the piece looked much more costly. "The stones are paste," volunteered the clerk by way of explanation and he offered to reserve the bracelet until George could return with the cash.

At home, Alice waited impatiently for George and her new bracelet. When he arrived there was a smug smile on his face: "Darling, you won't believe this, but I showed the bracelet to Oscar, the jeweller in Swiss Cottage, and he offered me £800 for it. Now I can buy you all three bracelets!"

When Alice recovered from her shock at this turn of events, she was near tears. "No, George, I have changed my mind. I don't want a bracelet. In fact, I don't want any birthday present at all." Explain.

Sudoku

			2	8			6	
1		6					4	
			1					
	6	1				4		
	4	5		3		7	9	
		9				8	2	
					3			
	5					9		7
	3			6	8			

```
E Y G C P A I G T E T I Y J W
S D E G N I H U I L N Y B O Z
O G A H G T N U E X P E R U W
H T R A M R C B B A L K C O T
Y E M E N E G H C R A S H H D
H L D N O N G R J B N T L O V
K E E A I I P W L E T L W A P
I C D V X O B E R I F D W E G
Y T I N K I N G T A B L E M Q
S R L I F T A F I R E P L U G
D O S A I U L I X T E U L Y X
Y D C N G H L T V D T E G U B
E E G E V F O W A S S D L I C
N O Z Z L E Y L O C K W E I R
T S Y P F F R E D L O H S A G
```

ACE	HINGED	PEDAL
ALLOY	HOSE	PLANT
ARCH	HUB	REEL
AXLE	INERTIA	RIG
DRIVING BELT	INGOT	SLAG
ELECTRODE	INKING TABLE	SLIDE
ERG	ION	STULM
FIREBOX	KEY	TIE
FIREPLUG	LIFT	TRAM
FIT	LOCK WEIR	UHF
GAS HOLDER	NOZZLE	VANE
GAUGE	NUT	VOLT
GEAR	PAWL	WORKABLE

Spot the difference

Can you spot ten differences between this pair of pictures?

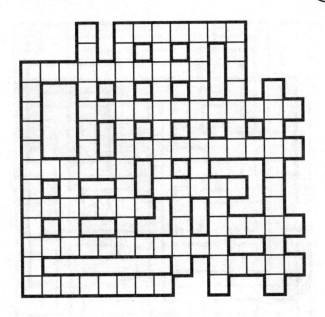

5 letter words
ANNUL
EMBED
ODDLY
PAYEE
UNSAY

6 letter words
EXODUS
FRESCO

7 letter words
ROBOTIC
SOMEDAY
Y-FRONTS

8 letter words
EXERCISE
PRINCESS

9 letter words
DISEMBODY
MOUSETRAP

10 letter words
CARBON SINK
STRIP CLUBS

11 letter words
QUANTUM LEAP
UNDERGROUND

12 letter words
CONTERMINOUS
SECOND COMING
SMALL FORTUNE

Maze

The numbers on the side and bottom of the grid indicate occupied squares or groups of consecutive occupied squares in each row or column. Can you finish the grid so that it contains one Key, two Amulets, three Cutlasses, four bars of Gold, and the numbers tally?

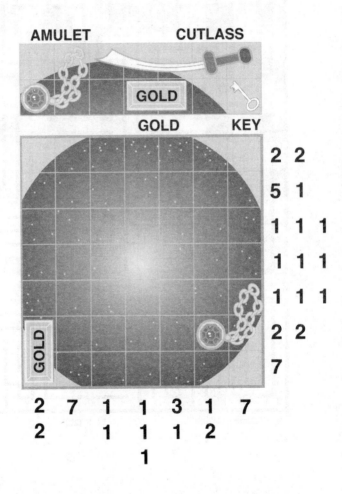

Crossword

Across

1. Smooch (4)
4. Arrangement (6)
7. Speck (4)
8. Hay roof (6)
9. Say again (7)
11. Newspaper (3)
13. Droop (3)
14. Touring home (7)
16. Precision (6)
18. Long-billed Egyptian bird (4)
19. Remove (6)
20. Way (4)

Down

2. Non-functional (11)
3. Detective (6)
4. Modelled (3)
5. Practise fighting (4)
6. Utterance (11)
10. British beverage (3)
12. Spa treatment (6)
15. Fool (4)
17. Fish eggs (3)

Sudoku

				9	3		4	
		9					6	
		5		7				
		1			4			6
7		6		3		5		9
9			8			1		
				8		6		
	6					2		
	8		3	1				

```
J M A D L L A B R E H T E T K
F O O T B A L L H B N E E R G
G O A L I E E T A L P E M O H
W F T K C O C E L T T U H S H
R R E F E R E E D I K S D B C
E A N W S I L L Y C T L B A T
T C N D E R E L U R E F M S I
T Q I R T C E P I I L O S K P
U U S W U V C K F O M F G E Z
P E D E A N E T G B U F N T R
I T D R B R U M P I R E I B E
R B T B A O P B A V C N N A K
O A U M S U V R H T S S N L N
N L J N E G G E O C C E I L U
C L O V E M A G R P T H P J B
```

BASE	INNINGS	REFEREE
BASKETBALL	IRON	RUN
BAT	LOVE	SCRUM
BUNKER	MATCH	SET
CLUB	NET	SHUTTLECOCK
DEUCE	OFFENSE	SILLY
FOOTBALL	OUTFIELD	STRIKER
GAME	OVER	TEE
GOALIE	PITCH	TENNIS
GOLF	PROP	TETHERBALL
GREEN	PUCK	TRAVEL
GUARD	PUTTER	UMPIRE
HOME PLATE	RACQUET BALL	WOOD

Drink-drive

With the festive season approaching, the chief of police ordered
a clampdown on drinking and driving. In line with the order,
two of his officers were keeping a discreet watch on an exclusive
downtown club when they saw a customer stagger out of the door
and fall down on the snow-covered ground. After a few seconds he
picked himself up, stumbled to his car and fumbled for the keys.
Eventually he got the door open and managed to start the car,
grinding the gears before moving off in a zigzag course.

The police car followed, stopped him and gave him a breathalyzer test. The test was negative. Obviously something was wrong with the equipment, as the man reeked of alcohol. The officers took him to the police station for another test. Again, negative. A blood test showed the same result. The police were baffled. Can you solve the mystery?

Spot the difference

Can you spot ten differences between this pair of pictures?

2			8			6		
					4	1		
			6	7	9		8	
						9	5	
4				2				1
	5	8						
	6		9	5	2			
		9	1					
		2			8			3

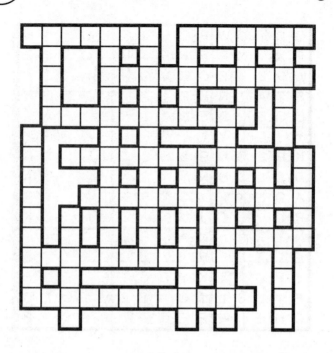

5 letter words
DITTO
ELVES
INERT
INSET
NOISE
RUMBA
SINUS

6 letter words
AZTECS
ERRATA

7 letter words
DEAD SET
DRESSER

9 letter words
CUSTOMARY
HARMONICA

11 letter words
INTRA-ATOMIC
REACTIONARY
SMALL SCREEN
SQUARE ROOTS
THEATRICALS

12 letter words
ARCTIC CIRCLE
SARSAPARILLA
SIAMESE TWINS
TRACE ELEMENT

Word search

```
G R I P W F G R X O L U R S H
F X I N R F I E J B A Q S E F
W P B B E O R V O U C A Z S A
S T A I N K P I X M R M U N N
O Q R L E E R L L B E I F A G
Y J D L Y L L O D L E G Z G Z
K R E S N G B S O E V G U S B
D S L I D N Y Y R K Y S B B A
A Q L K F I C Y R E T X I Y R
R U J E E J N X W E M M I C K
N I F S A N A I R R E O G M I
E L J L E R N L U Q C H B O S
Y P U J I K Y D G T E K C U B
F I P S L T G Y E B M O D L D
Q H E E P E E G O O R C S D B
```

BARDELL	FIPS	NANCY
BARKIS	FLITE	OLIVER
BILL SIKES	GRIP	OMER
BRASS	GUSTER	PIP
BUCKET	HEEP	PRIG
BUD	JENNY	QUILP
BUMBLE	JINGLE	RUDGE
BUZFUZ	JO	SCROOGE
CHEERYBLE	JUPE	SLEARY
DARNEY	KROOK	SNAGSBY
DOLLY	LA CREEVY	WEMMICK
DOMBEY	MIGGS	WINKLE
FANG	MOULD	WREN

Sudoku

			4	7			8	3
	2	9	1					
				5				2
	6							9
		3		4		5		
1							2	
5				1				
					4	7	6	
8	1			3	9			

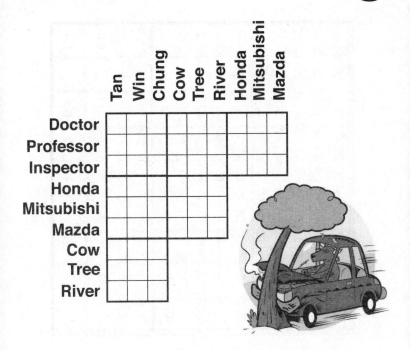

A Doctor, a Professor and a Police Inspector all made insurance claims after minor accidents. Can you work out who is who, what car they were driving, and what they bumped into?

1) The Doctor, not a Mitsubishi driver, hit a tree.
2) Chung didn't hit a cow in his Mazda and isn't a policeman.
3) The cow was hit by a Honda, not driven by Win or the Inspector.

Word search

```
J Y D L E I F G N I R P S R H
O N O I D R E A G A N A E J B
H N L O U A Q L N O X I N L S
N S E H G U H O V J F O D D E
S B A R I O S M C I S M C Y E
O A G E Q K R R E P S R A S Z
N N Q N R R O D M R O G T N I
N K T A I S S I O W L A A O A
I S L A B K S N B N F E P O H
N C L Y D D E E T A R M E O C
N S A D G A N Y N B U L T P E
O N E S L N S E M L W L T D L
S B S E Y O U Q K O G A Y O L
A O W R N N O O W W J B K G I
M V O K I N H S Y R A B B G V
```

ABLOW	ELVIS	PELE
ASH	ESTAFAN	PETTY
BALL	GAYE	REAGAN
BANKS	GORDON	RENO
BARYSHNIKOV	HUGHES	ROSS
BENNY	JOHNSON	SADAT
CLARKSON	LEE	SEAL
CROSBY	MASON	SIMPSON
CROW	MOSS	SNOOOP DOGG
DAHMER	NESS	SPRINGFIELD
DION	NIXON	TYSON
DOLE	O'NEAL	VILLECHAIZE

Across

7. Inauspicious (11)
8. Pure booze (7)
10. Intuition (5)
12. Payback (5)
13. Normal (7)
17. Royal decoration (5, 6)

Down

1. Christmastide (4)
2. Kabul's currency (7)
3. Small bird (4)
4. Inuit boot (6)
5. Pinch (3)
6. Caviar whale (6)
9. Feared (7)
10. Croupe (6)
11. Self-targeting (6)
14. Desire (4)
15. Simple (4)
16. Period (3)

Sudoku

	4		7				3	1
		6	3					9
						5	2	
		1						
3		8		2		1		5
						3		
	6	2						
4					8	7		
8	7				9		6	

Spot the difference

Can you spot ten differences between this pair of pictures?

```
S P I R I T X I F C A T T T X
Y E N V R H R N L T U B E E R
S Y V E S I D A I S L U L Q G
Z W D A S J R E P P H S M V H
D I M H R E G Q A P A H I I F
C S T B T G O N V A K E G N A
L U A A C E P E A N A R U O W
J S E E C H Y I K H C R X R C
S T Y T S S A U E C C Y J D B
Y A A T H O U B O S A U Z I C
A V R E R C R M K L L S T N M
K A U S U K S A E E W T A A A
O C M I B Q F R P Y E I J I C
T E N N O B U D I R Z B N R O
R A T A F I A G S K C S D E N
```

ALE	FLIP	ROSE
ANISETTE	GIMLET	RUM
BASS	GRAVES	RYE
BEER	IRISH	SACK
BITTERS	JULEP	SCHNAPPS
CAVA	KAHLUA	SHERRY
CHA	KAVA	SHRUB
CIDER	KIRSCH	SMASH
CLARET	MACON	SPIRIT
CRU	MUSCAT	TEA
DRAMBUIE	NOG	TOKAY
DUBONNET	PEKOE	VIN ORDINAIRE
FIX	RATAFIA	WINE

					3			6
	2				8			
5	1			4				
	3	1				8		
8	9			1			2	5
		6				7	1	
				2			3	9
			8				6	
1			7					

Crossword

Across

1. Coffee jockey (7)
4. Swamp (3)
6. Snow sport enthusiast (5)
7. Greek S (5)
8. Pair (3)
9. Conventions (5)
12. Form (5)
13. Electric discharge (3)
15. Empower (5)
17. Less wet (5)
18. Jigger (3)
19. Gilt (7)

Down

1. Founded (5)
2. Devastating (7)
3. Mêlée (9)
4. Large (3)
5. Secretor (5)
7. Give up (9)
10. Staying power (7)
11. Subsist (5)
14. Hex (5)
16. Merely (3)

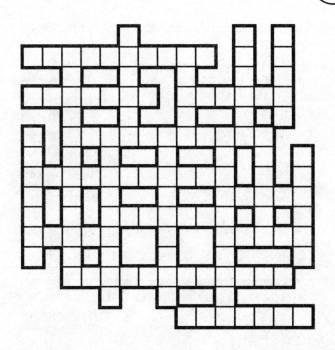

5 letter words
COWER
HOO-HA
STRAP
USHER
UTTER

6 letter words
DEPORT
HAUNCH
STENCH
WEALTH
YARROW

7 letter words
DIFFUSE
EPISTLE
MIRRORS
OBLIQUE

9 letter words
GRAFFITIS
TEST DRIVE

10 letter words
PERSECUTOR
PICARESQUE

11 letter words
LORD'S PRAYER
ORTHOGRAPHY

12 letter words
CHIROPRACTIC
CIVILISATION

Spot the difference

Can you spot ten differences between this pair of pictures?

4	3	1						
			8		6			
8		6			2			
		2			9			3
6				3				7
5			1			2		
			6			1		4
			9		7			
						7	6	2

Mirror image

Only one of these pictures is an exact mirror image of the first one. Can you spot it?

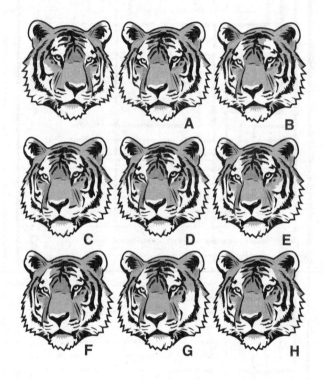

Box it

The value of each shape is the number of sides each shape has, multiplied by the number within it. Thus a square containing the number 4 has a value of 16. Find a block of four squares (two squares wide by two squares high) with a total value of exactly 100.

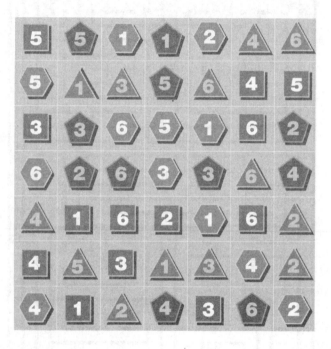

```
V L I L A C I N O R E V Q S J
D I O V X W T E H E S U E H Z
E N O M E N A O D D A V I E A
V A E L L A T E P D E L P P L
X C L M A T L Y H A S M O H D
K A D L O W P K L L T M U E S
A N H N E P U P O S R T E R T
I N I I O G H L X B A W R D A
N A S P I C I I E O E A I S P
O S O X E Y E N L C H Y G P E
G E S U H T N A C A S B E U L
E S O R I E W R Q J A L R R I
B A X M T R H I J L I A O S A
Z M F L A G I A M L E D N E D
S E P A L Y N S Y A V E N S P
```

ACANTHUS	HEART'S-EASE	PINK
ALOE	HOTTONIA	POPPY
ANEMONE	IRIS	ROSE
ARUM	JACOB'S LADDER	SEPAL
ASPIC	LILAC	SESAME
AVENS	LILY	SHEPHERD'S PURSE
BALM	LINARIA	STAPELIA
BEGONIA	MAY	TWAYBLADE
BENNET	NEMOPHILA	VERONICA
CANNA	NIGELLA	VIOLA
EDELWEISS	OX-EYE	WEED
ERIGERON	PETAL	WHIN
FLAG	PHLOX	WOLD

Spot the difference

Can you spot ten differences between this pair of pictures?

Crossword

Across

2. Inlet (4)
4. Upstart (7)
5. Bitter hickory tree (6)
7. Russian ruler (4)
8. Harvest (4)
9. Flick through (4)
11. Wooden shoe (4)
14. Sack (6)
15. Sultry (7)
16. Error (4)

Down

1. Marriage bans? (3-3)
2. Extremist sect (4)
3. Entry permit (4)
4. Grace (5)
6. Test (5)
9. Nib (6)
10. Dreadful (5)
12. Breather (4)
13. Puff (4)

In the area

Can you work out the approximate area that this boat is occupying?

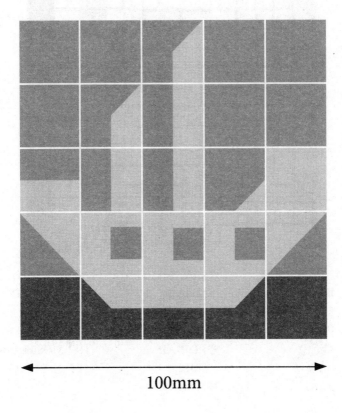

100mm

Word grid

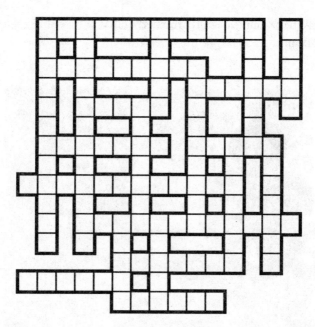

5 letter words
DATUM
EVENS
FLORA
LEAFY
TAROT
TRAIT

6 letter words
EDITOR
FAR-OFF
YAMMER

7 letter words
ANTIGEN
EARTHEN
ECHELON
ORDINAL
STRIPED
SUBSIDY

9 letter words
EASY CHAIR
REDDENING

12 letter words
BULLDOG CLIPS
CLUB SANDWICH
TEST-TUBE BABY
THERMOS FLASK
TITTLE-TATTLE

The balls below have been rearranged. Can you work out the new sequence of the balls from the clues given below?

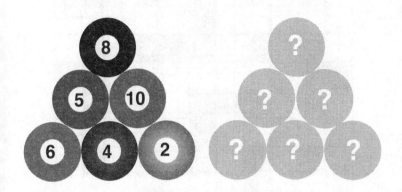

The 10 ball is immediately to the right of the 4.
The 6 ball isn't touching the 8 or the 2.
The 5 ball is touching the 10 but not the 4.
The two second row balls total less than the top one.

Crossword

Across

5. Accused (7)
7. Spanish noble (3)
8. Show again (5)
9. Superior (5)
10. Ignore (7)
14. Hyper (5)
16. Spacious (5)
17. Regret (3)
18. Gather together (7)

Down

1. Heft (5)
2. Creamy punch (6)
3. Wood-shaper (4)
4. Go inside (5)
6. Specs on a stick (9)
7. Flotsam (9)
11. Severe scolding (6)
12. Protect (5)
13. Bodily humour (5)
15. Round, thickly-curled hairdo (4)

Spot the difference

Can you spot ten differences between this pair of pictures?

The runner

The crowd in the stadium were on their feet, cheering and clapping. It was the end of the 10,000 metres race in the world championships. Jonathan Cansino was leading the field and looked certain to take the medal. He was 3 metres from the finish when the runner from Nigeria passed him and crossed the line. Jonathan glanced across in horror, which quickly turned to jubilation, and threw his arms up in triumph.

What had happened?

Word grid

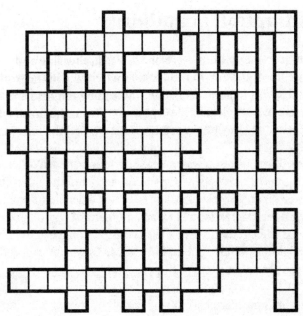

5 letter words
ADIEU
ENNUI
ONION
SINCE
TAPIR
TOKEN

6 letter words
ASK FOR
STRING

7 letter word
WAYSIDE

8 letter words
ATHENEUM
MEPHITIC

9 letter words
GO-GETTING
ROBOTLIKE

10 letter words
AMPERE-TURN
MULTIMEDIA

11 letter words
BLOODSUCKER
DISHEVELLED
INQUISITION

12 letter words
ALL-EMBRACING
JE NE SAIS QUOI

Presumption of authority

Lee Dawson was 15 minutes early for his appointment with Stuart Gaylord, junior partner in Mitchell, Rosenbloom, O'Leary, Saffran & Loeb. He was requested to await the appointed time although he could observe through the glass partition that Gaylord was sitting at his desk doing nothing except puffing a cigar.

At 3 p.m. sharp, Dawson was ushered into the panelled office, where Gaylord greeted him with a limp handshake without rising. Offering his client a cigar, he rocked back in his chair, balancing perilously and giving the impression that at any moment he could fall either way. More of a circus act than a legal consultation, Lee thought with some irritation. "What can I do for you, Mr Dawson?" asked Gaylord condescendingly, prepared to dispense jurisprudential wisdom.

Lee Dawson's problem had started with the sale of his stamp collection, but Gaylord let him tell the story in his own words: "I did not know the buyer and therefore I insisted on cash in the amount of $42,000. The same morning I made my way to the Madison Avenue branch of my bank to deposit the funds to the credit of my account. This branch, like most, is organized on the open-plan basis. Having filled in the deposit slip, I approached one of the desks, occupied apparently by George Appleby, vice-president. At this bank everybody but the doorman is a vice-president. Appleby counted the money, initialled the slip and I departed. When I received the statement of my account in due course, there was no $42,000 credit. I visited the bank, produced the paying-in slip to the branch manager, who pointed out that it was not stamped and that the initials were not recognized. After further enquiries, it transpired that Vice-President Appleby had been out for lunch at the time in question and probably a tired customer had sat down at his desk for a brief rest. One of Appleby's

colleagues was able to give a description of the stranger to the police, but the bank denies liability. What do I do now?"

Gaylord, still in balancing mode, decided to play it safe and adopted a normal sitting position. "You have nothing to worry about, Mr Dawson. There was a test case a few years ago and the court decided that the doctrine of presumed authority applies. You had every right to assume that the person sitting at that desk was acting for the bank and therefore the bank is undoubtedly liable.

They might still go to court as a matter of principle in the hope of upsetting the previous judgement, but they don't have a chance. If you decide to proceed, we shall be happy to act for you." During the court hearing 14 months later, the judge upheld the presumption of authority doctrine. Nevertheless because of the statement of one witness, he found for the defence and the case was dismissed.

Can you guess what the witness testified?

Sale of the year

Berner's department store in North Finchley held their annual sale, which was considered a social event in all the surrounding districts. Prices were marked down by as much as 50 per cent and for some items as much as 70 per cent.

Queues were forming by 5 a.m. for opening at 9 a.m. By that time the line stretched almost around the whole block. Just before opening time a man arrived by taxi and immediately pushed himself to the front of the queue. Angry shouts sent him back toward the end of the line-up. He did not utter a word and his pleading look was to no avail. He tried again, but angry voices and veiled threats forced him to retreat. On his third attempt he was physically attacked and pushed from the pavement.

After he recovered his composure, he took a piece of paper from his pocket and wrote a few lines, which he showed to the people next to him. Whatever he wrote spread like wildfire throughout the queue, resulting in a great deal of amusement and some embarrassment.

What do you think the note said?

Crossword

Across

7. Give off (7)
8. Since (3)
9. Heavy (5)
10. Outline (5)
11. Downtrodden (9)
16. Strip (5)
18. Spree (5)
20. Louse (3)
21. Body burn (7)

Down

1. False target (5)
2. Portal (4)
3. Job path (6)
4. Cried (4)
5. Cope (6)
6. 3pm canonically (5)
12. Braids (6)
13. Figured out (6)
14. Sightless (5)
15. Star (5)
17. Journalist (4)
19. Distant (4)

Word search

```
I A N I P A Y L W M O O Q M X
N A I P U T I E A T O K A D O
T A X U O I S N T E C D E N F
N L H R N P C A C R K E T A H
A A K A E A W P O A R U M O U
I C W N I A C E H C S I Z L R
U A A Y D D H U C C A E B B O
Q L H R A C A S A M E W L E N
N U O M A H A R I R C C R U E
O F M P C P O H A H A E R P E
G A A M Z R A K S Y K G T O N
L N A C A Y I H U A D E M Z W
A Y O A N R P G O G W R W E A
A D E N A O A F U E G I A N H
A T O A R A P A W N E E S X S
```

ADENA	CROW	OLMEC
ALACALUFAN	DAKOTA	OMAHA
ALGONQUIAN	ERIE	ONEIDA
APACHE	FOX	OTTAWA
APINAI	FUEGIAN	PAWNEE
ARAPAHOE	HAIDA	PONCA
ARAUCAN	HURON	PUEBLOAN
ARIKAREE	INCA	SHAWNEE
ATOARA	LENAPE	SIOUX
AZTEC	MAYA	SIWASH
CAYUGA	MIAMI	TUPIAN
CHOCTAW	MOHAWK	TUSCARORA
CREE	NAZCA	WEA

Word grid

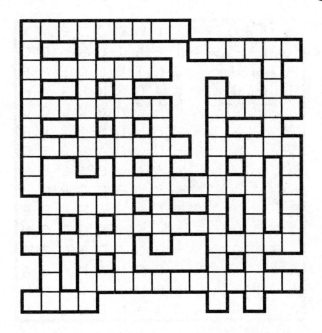

4 letter word
ISLE

5 letter words
COACH
REFER
TITAN
VEGAN

6 letter words
AWHILE
CACHET

CHASMS
CODIFY
EUNUCH
FORAGE
RETURN

8 letter words
ATTEMPTS
DWELLING
ENFORCED
EYE TOOTH
TELEVISE

9 letter words
FIELD TRIP
REST-CURES
SNARE DRUM
SWEETMEAT

12 letter words
LABOUR-SAVING
OVERNIGHT BAG
PICK UP THE TAB

HARD
PUZZLES

		5		9	6		3	
	3		1	8			9	
						8		
	7		3		8			
4		3		1			5	
	9		5		4			
						1		
	8		7	4			2	
		4		5	1		6	

Crossword

Across

6. Unending (9)
7. Fix (3)
8. Bucketload (3)
9. Paranormal power (3)
11. Ooze (7)
13. Plenty (3)
14. Dog foot (3)
16. Spruce (3)
17. Spinal bit (9)

Down

1. Magical (8)
2. Pinnacle (4)
3. Scoot (4)
4. Cruel person (6)
5. Sacred building (6)
10. Suppurating (8)
11. Lampoon (6)
12. Chopper (6)
15. Ardent (4)
16. Sate (4)

```
I F D R O N E O W X K W K F B
N O M E G A F A E I E J S L O
O J J S E E R K S C N O P U R
R E T R E U R R J A A A I K U
E X T K R T A A R E R H R O S
M K A S T R I A N D A O I S A
I U S O X A M L R O T I D E I
H T T V R A O T U M G X O R I
C Z B T M L S S G A M M N T B
M O P U K U C H I P U I P L E
K O T E M H S J I R M E L O A
G H L I U C O T O O A A A T S
I A N H T L E G N L Z N N O T
D A R V E Y J O R A H F T X Q
Z A P M M B I O R I V T I L O
```

ACE	GARM	NIMON
ANIMUS	GELTH	OGRI
AXOS	HOIX	OMEGA
BEAST	KASTRIAN	OOD
BOK	KRAAL	OPTRA
BORUSA	LAZAR	OSIRAN
CHIMERON	LUKOSER	RANI
CHIP	MAGS	SEER
CHULA	MARA	SPIRIDON PLANT
DALEK	MUTE	TARAN
DARVEY	MUTHI	TLOTOXL
DRONE	MUTO	TREE
EDITOR	MUTT	YETI

15	11	7	10		18	4	10	17	13	10	10	7
11		13		15		13		6		3		23
11	22	18	15	18	17	10		18	2	17	10	7
24		2		17		23		9		18		23
21	18	12	17	23	6	3	19	9	9	16	10	
23				15		11		16		11		23
5	11	7	18	20	10		25	10	2	2	10	16
1		19		23		4		17				7
	7	24	23	2	17	16	23	7	23	1	16	10
23		2		7		10		18		23		24
8	19	11	7	23		24	10	4	14	4	16	10
19		25		12		18		26		11		12
23	16	25	24	10	17	4	11		18	2	25	11

1 B	2 N	3	4	5	6	7	8	9	10	11	12	13
14	15	16	17	18	19	20	21	22	23 A	24	25	26

Riddle

The surgeon

A well-dressed man in his forties, let's call him John, enters a bar in Manhattan. After looking around, he sits down next to a shabbily-dressed man who is obviously the worse for drink. John strikes up a conversation and orders more drinks.

After some small talk, John makes the following proposition to the stranger: "I am Dr John Hopkins and I am a qualified surgeon. If you let me amputate your left forearm, I will pay you $100,000 and will provide you with an artificial limb." After some hesitation, the stranger agrees and they proceed to John's surgery.

After the amputation, John packs the limb in dry ice and sends the parcel to an address in Los Angeles. At the same time, he sends cables to a number of addresses on the West Coast. Several days later, six men meet in LA. The parcel is being opened, the men look at it, express satisfaction and disperse after burying the limb.

Find an explanation for this which will logically meet the circumstances.

Deal of the year

Frank Forrester's weekend treat was to read all sections of
the *Sunday Times* in bed from the first line to the last,
including the advertisements. When he came to the
classified ads section he noticed something which struck
him like a bolt from the blue.

He went to a dealer and, after much haggling, bought
something for £1,600. The next day he visited his friend
Bruce Miller, who had made his millions in the rag trade,
and offered him the same item for £35,000. Bruce did not
hesitate, paid cash and had the look of a man who had just
secured the bargain of his life. A week later he gave it to his
wife as a birthday present and she seemed thrilled beyond
words.

Sadly, she had a fatal accident in her Rolls-Royce Corniche
shortly thereafter. Bruce had the car repaired and, in the
circumstances, was only too anxious to get rid of it. As the
car was 12 years old, he got only £30,000 – more or less
the market price – but strangely enough, this included the
birthday present to his wife.

What do you make of it?

Every tree ▲ has one tent △ found horizontally or vertically adjacent to it. No tent can be in an adjacent square to another tent (even diagonally). The numbers by each row and column tell you how many tents are there. Can you locate all the tents?

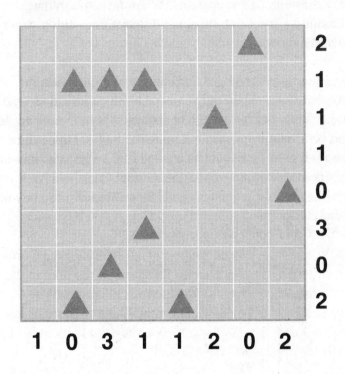

Lost luggage

Alan Goide was proud of his Hartmann luggage, which he had bought at Harrods. He always travelled with a full set and although he had crossed the Atlantic more than 20 times during the last 12 months, the luggage looked like new. Quality shows!

Alan had just arrived at the Park Lane Hotel, Central Park South, after a supersonic Concorde trip from London. After a quick shower he wanted to unpack when he noticed that the combination would not open the lock on the largest case. He was just about to try and find a locksmith when he received a telephone call: "Mr Goide, I'm glad I've found you. I was a co-passenger on Concorde and I have one of your Hartmann cases, while I presume you have one of mine. Can I come along to exchange?"

Alan Goide was relieved, and soon thereafter a hotel bellboy brought up his suitcase, trading it for the other. He was slightly amused as the same mistake had happened to him before and was bound to occur to many Hartmann owners. Later, over a relaxing drink in the bar, he pondered over how quickly the other passenger had been able to contact him. Probably through British Airways, he mused, when suddenly a thought struck him which made him contact the police. What came into his mind?

Sudoku

				8		3		5
	6				5	9	1	
2								
			6	1			4	
		5		2		1		
	3			5	7			
								9
	1	2	8				6	
6		4		7				

11	18	24	20			8	2	21	3	3	13	21	20
12		17		10		4		4		21		6	
4	22	16	12	21	11	15		1	15	12	18	22	
16		18		10		22		21		12		18	
26	24	14		4	23	6	24	25	5	21	23		
4				23		8				17		5	
23	6	6	16	18	7		10	18	7	14	18	7	
13		22				4		9				4	
	5	21	22	19	24	13	5	24		23	4	17	
5		17		21		21		21		4		25	
24	19	6	4	5		22	21	17	21	22	24	22	
19		24		5		19		18		18		21	
4	25	25	18	25	25	6	7		25	12	4	5	

1	2	3 Z	4	5	6	7 R	8	9	10	11	12 L	13
14	15	16	17	18	19	20	21	22	23	24	25	26

Across

1. For fear that (4)
4. Thumped (6)
7. Exoskeleton (8)
8. Threaded fastener (5)
10. Slash (5)
11. Venture (5)
13. Manservant (5)
16. Illegal boarder (8)
18. Go back (6)
19. Assist (4)

Down

2. Epoch (3)
3. Badger (5)
4. Twinge (4)
5. Supervisory serf (5)
6. Road reflector (7)
9. Little act (7)
12. Tight-twisted cotton (5)
14. Soaking (5)
15. Only (4)
17. Hole punch (3)

Word search

```
Z N E D L W S E N Y U G T O H
O E U Y X A U D R E Y V A N D
S M O L W Q A N U E F A L O M
M Y N J S U E P F S F B F A L
A H Y A P H H E U S A T R T S
E S B H R R Y L H N E G O M I
N M I P O I L R I R A S J E L
A N I N Z I E R E R O S I R I
S Y I L C W A L E G O W E R U
T U P U I M S T Y G Q L O F S
S I L V I A I B O E U T Y C W
J G E J D R A E R O S D W A B
K O U S X D H Y K E U O L I W
L N G N R E T S N E D L I U G
O M A H S N B B S U L A C S E
```

AENAS	ESCALUS	MARGARET
AGUE	EUPHRONIUS	MARINA
AMBAS	GAOL	NESTOR
ARDEN	GOWER	NYM
ARIEL	GUILDENSTERN	SHREW
AUDREY	GUYNES	SILIUS
BAWD	IMOGEN	SILVIA
CAIUS	IRAS	SNUG
DAUPHIN	IRIS	THAISA
ELY	JUNO	TYRE
EMILIA	LAFEU	WALL
EROS	LUCILLUS	WYE

Sudoku

		1	3					
2		8	9					4
	9						7	
			8		6			2
		5		7		4		
6			5		1			
	2						5	
1					4	8		3
					3	1		

Only two of these pictures are exactly the same. Can you spot the matching pair?

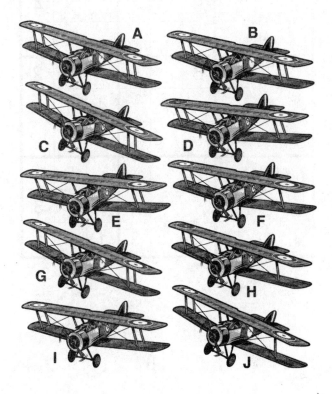

Camp conifer

Every tree 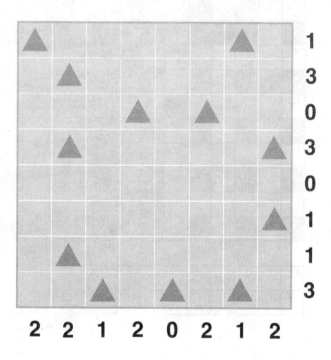 has one tent △ found horizontally or vertically adjacent to it. No tent can be in an adjacent square to another tent (even diagonally). The numbers by each row and column tell you how many tents are there. Can you locate all the tents?

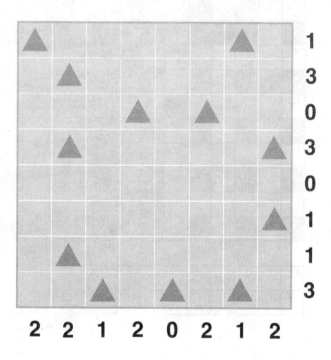

	26		1		26		15		26		22	
22	20	12	5	3	13		7	6	19	10	19	16
	16		3		6		13		8		10	
25	6	2	14		7	15	6	8	3	6	16	6
	13				4		2		19		19	
18	22	22	18	26	19	7		3	2	11	5	19
			21		2		13		11			
19	13	11	19	19		26	19	21	19	16	15	5
	19		16		26		2				2	
24	15	26	26	11	5	19	1		24	3	26	12
	4		6		6		18		15		9	
24	16	15	17	19	2		5	18	9	23	19	12
	19		19		4		23		5		16	

1	2	3	4 G	5	6	7	8	9	10	11	12	13
14	15	16	17	18	19 E	20	21	22 P	23	24	25	26

The hijack

Shortly after 11 a.m. one October morning, two men were busy
unloading a shipment of dresses in Manhattan's garment district.
As they opened the back door of their delivery truck, three men
approached them, one brandishing an Uzi submachine gun, forced
them back into the truck, handcuffed them, and locked them in.

No one passing by noticed the incident to report it to the police,
nor did the police have any prior information of the planned hijack.
Nevertheless, two 5th Precinct officers were on the lookout for
the truck as it approached the entrance to the Manhattan Bridge
and after spotting it they took up a pursuit that ended when the
raiders crashed in Brooklyn. Assuming that the police had no other
reason to stop or pursue the vehicle, how do you account for their
remarkable success in apprehending the hijackers?

Radar

The numbers in some cells in the grid indicate the exact number of black cells that should border it. Shade these black, until all the numbers are surrounded by the correct number of black cells.

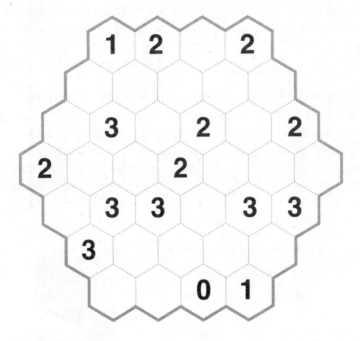

```
D L T S I N I V L A C N Y O B
E A Z O C L E A N G J A C O B
M I N N L I K E Y L D A E D A
E N A M A M M O N T A M O X B
E E Y A I B D N S C J V A G N
D V E D U O D A U H U T E G C
E B L A O G L M M N E R O R I
R Y S M A R O T A W C R S K R
U E E R R A N C Y N T I S E E
P D W S O D O M C H N B O X D
A S U R S U M C O R D A P G E
X S H I V A E D S H A M A N S
F E R T M L O V H J O N A H W
L L E H C X L U E M O R T A L
S I S T E R T E R E F A H W V
```

ADAM	HELL	ORTHODOX
CALVINIST	JACOB	PAX
CLEAN	JONAH	REDEEMED
COSHER	KOSHER	ROTA
CURSED	LAST DAY	SEDER
DEADLY	LAVER	SHIVA
DEAN	LIMBO	SISTER
DOOMED	LOT	SODOM
ERRANCY	MAGI	SURSUM CORDA
ESAU	MAMMON	TEREFAH
EVE	MANNA	TREF
GRADUAL	MORTAL	VENIAL
HAMAN	NUNCIO	WESLEYAN

		6		9		4		
		7						
8	9				4		7	3
					2		9	7
7						1		
		3	8				5	
4				8				5
		8	6		3			
		2	4			3		

Crossword

Across

1. Hem in (5)
4. Tall Canadian tree (5)
7. Shape of UFOs? (6)
8. Satisfy (4)
10. Sticking together (8)
12. Ready (8)
15. Skim swiftly (4)
16. Place (6)
17. Musical phrase (5)
18. Used up (5)

Down

1. Deep singer (5)
2. Metal fastener (4)
3. Non-drinker (8)
5. Gold-bearing gravel (6)
6. Upright (5)
9. I will start now (4, 4)
11. Win over (6)
12. Postulate (5)
13. Open (5)
14. Price reduction (4)

Treasure island

The numbers on the side and bottom of the grid indicate occupied squares or groups of consecutive occupied squares in each row or column. Can you finish the grid so that it contains two Keys, two Amulets, three Cutlasses and three bars of Gold, and the numbers tally?

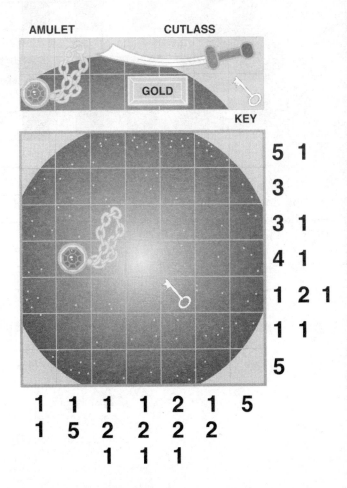

Logic sequence

The balls below have been rearranged. Can you work out the new sequence of the balls from the clues given below?

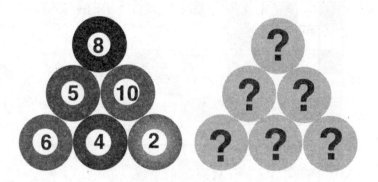

The 10 ball is below the 4.

The bottom row adds up to 19.

The 5 ball is touching only the 2 and 6

The 6 ball is immediately to the left of the 5

1	2	3	4	5	6	7	8	9	10	11 W	12	13
14 F	15	16	17	18	19	20	21	22	23 T	24	25	26

The experiment

Alex was working on an important experiment. Unfortunately, through his carelessness, the experiment was a complete failure. Yet strangely enough, Alex – who was comparatively unknown in his profession – became a world celebrity because of his negligence.

Explain.

```
C H R O N A P L I T E N E C N
Q A O Z I A D O N T O P M A I
H E L C M M A B L T J N E R O
Y L E U A M B L P Y A P R O R
A B R D R M E E L P I T T T G
L A C E N E L D P A A M A O I
I C R N K O I E N U C B I L L
T O F O E S T F Q E X T D D I
E N I G E I E A I G L I I D E
C O A R R L R H T D A B V T Q
A M R E W A C K E L O A I U E
J S D B P R T U O N O M L A R
U N I U A L S G N S D I E N E
I O L I G O P E L I C D D D D
N E D Y N A N H E D R O N C A
```

ABELITE	CAJU	INDERITE
ACENE	CAROTOL	LEPTON
ADER	CDNA	LIGROIN
ADONT	CHRON	MONOCABLE
ALLACTITE	DEMODIFIER	NAPPE
ALMON	DIALOG	NUCLEOR
ALURE	DIARCH	OLIGOPELIC
AMIDO	DIATREME	ONDE
AMIN	DIENE	PARAQUAT
ANHEDRON	ERGON	PNPN
APLITE	ESKER	POLYIMIDE
BION	FIARD	TSPN
BLENDE	HYALITE	WACKE

Sudoku

		4					2	
8	2			5	4			
2	1		5			6	8	
	8		4		6			7
7	4		2			9	3	
6	9			3	8			
		5					9	

Dusk or dawn?

Norman Bronstein, a sports enthusiast and loner, would try anything that presented a physical challenge of endurance and danger. On this occasion, white-water rafting in the Amazon, he set off alone from Manaus one winter morning. At first all went well, but early in the afternoon his raft entered some rapids and struck a rock; Norman was thrown clear onto the shore. His raft and all belongings, including his pocket watch, were lost. He lay for days, unconscious from a head wound. When he finally came to, it was twilight. Although dazed, Norman realized that it was dusk and that he would have to spend another night before he could be rescued. How did he know instantly that it was dusk, not dawn?

Crossword

Across

1. Stop slouching (3, 2)
4. Smallest (5)
7. Park officer (6)
8. Shafted ball weapon (4)
10. Form the base (8)
12. Cleaning solution (8)
15. Ship's jail (4)
16. Musical composition (6)
17. Calcite (5)
18. Napped leather (5)

Down

1. Shoulder gesture (5)
2. Hue (4)
3. Gravid (8)
5. Worth farming (6)
6. Idea (5)
9. Ample (8)
11. Eye receptor (6)
12. Three-dimensional (5)
13. Interest (5)
14. Appointment (4)

The pearl necklace

Caroline was a salaried companion to Margaret Stenton, the wealthy widow of a media tycoon.

One day, window-shopping on 5th Avenue, Mrs Stenton saw a beautiful pearl necklace in Harry Winston's window. She decided that she had to have it. They asked for Winston, an old friend of the family, who had the necklace brought in. The pearls were of an exquisite pink hue and Caroline thought it was the most beautiful piece of jewellery she had ever seen. Harry Winston assured Margaret the pearls were not cultured but those for which pearl divers in the Bay of Bengal spend their lives looking.

One weekend when Margaret Stenton was out of town, Caroline was invited to a ball by her fiancé. She borrowed one of Margaret's gowns, for which she had permission, and also took the pearl necklace from the safe, for which she had no permission.

In the underground car park of the hotel where the ball was being held she was mugged and robbed of the necklace and her handbag. Caroline was devastated. Her first impulse was to contact the police and confess to Mrs Stenton that she had taken the necklace from the safe without permission. She quickly changed her mind. The necklace was not insured and if she had told the police and Mrs Stenton, they might have suspected a conspiracy and that she had arranged the mugging herself. Caroline was now in a state of utter panic.

She immediately contacted Harry Winston and asked him if he could supply a replacement identical to the original. He confirmed that he could do this but it would cost a small fortune. Caroline withdrew all her savings and borrowed the rest from her fiancé and friends. She collected the replacement necklace, which she promptly put back in the safe.

This unfortunate incident completely wrecked Caroline's life. In spite of extreme economy she was unable to repay the loan on time. Her friends deserted her and her fiancé broke off the engagement.

A few years later Mrs Stenton was due to attend a function and invited Caroline to accompany her. She then uttered one sentence to her employee, which made her go white and break down in floods of tears.

What did she say?

Crossword

Across

1. Platter (4)
3. Coinage (6)
8. Pole (3)
9. Oratorio (7)
10. Of same category (8)
12. Representative law suit (4, 4)
14. Set aside (7)
15. Dock (3)
17. Bright (6)
18. Oven-cook (4)

Down

1. Social entrant (3)
2. Hallowed place (6)
4. Rudimentary down (10)
5. Bye (4)
6. Migrant (7)
7. Go faster (10)
10. Hearty (7)
11. Greek L (6)
13. Hand out (4)
16. Scrapie, but for cows (3)

Sudoku

5		4					6	
							4	8
			6		2	7		
				1	8	4		
9				5				3
		2	9	3				
		7	3		4			
8	3							
	1					9		7

Nelson's column

Rudolf Mueller from Dusseldorf arrived in London on his first trip abroad. He wanted to see as much as a four-day stay would permit and was particularly interested in famous sights, including the Tower of London, Madame Tussaud's, Trafalgar Square and Nelson's Column. Needless to say, he included Buckingham Palace and the Changing of the Guards in his plans.

Back at his hotel in Sussex Gardens, he studied all the tourist pamphlets to acquaint himself with the historical background. He read that the Tower of London was built in 1078 and that Nelson's Column was erected to celebrate the famous victory at Trafalgar, and that it was 170 feet high. This meant nothing to Rudolf as he was used to the metric system. Remembering from his school days that three feet equalled one yard, and that one yard was approximately equal to one metre, he pencilled in, next to a photograph of the column, 56 metres. Sadly, his inaccurate calculation cost the life of his best friend.

Explain.

Luxury cruise

It is easy to make friends during a transatlantic crossing, but such friendships seldom survive the five days from Southampton to New York.

The following took place during the third evening on the *Queen Mary*. After dinner and a few rounds of bridge, a small but select group gathered for drinks and small talk at the bar on the promenade deck. The group included a real-estate tycoon – Robert Waterman – and his secretary Madame Croiseau and her toy-boy, plus Count Orlando and his beautiful wife Elisabeth. Fred Gerrard, the renowned jeweller, was entertaining the party with stories of famous diamonds and their fate.

He told of the great Mogul found in 1650 in India, which weighed 787 carats. The Orloff was stolen by a French soldier, bought by Prince Orloff and given to Catherine the Great of Russia. The most famous of them all, the Koh-i-nor, changed hands many times and was acquired by the British in 1849. Possibly the most fascinating story concerned the affair of the diamond necklace, the scandal at the court of Louis XVI in 1785, which discredited the French monarchy and, according to Napoleon, was one of the major causes of the French Revolution.

The conversation then turned to the high cost of insuring precious stones. To solve the problem, jewels were kept in a bank vault and instead replicas were worn by the owners. Waterman was of the opinion that these imitations were of such excellent quality that only the closest expert examination would discover the fake. Fred Gerrard begged to differ and maintained that the trained eye would know the difference at arm's length. This statement was met with disbelief by everyone.

To prove his point, Gerrard looked at Madame Croiseau's diamond bracelet and without hesitation described it as a superb imitation. To alleviate her obvious embarrassment, he added, "Madame, I am sure that the real thing is safe and sound in the ship's vault." A slight nod from Madame confirmed his diagnosis. The round of subdued applause acknowledged the expertise.

"On the other hand," he continued, "the Countess's necklace is one of the most exquisite pieces of jewellery I have seen for some time." The Countess visibly blushed and looked at Gerrard with a strange expression. The Count smiled with obvious satisfaction. "This time you are mistaken, dear boy." "Impossible," retorted the jeweller. "Would you care to wager, say $500?" said the Count. Gerrard accepted, and the Countess handed him the necklace for closer examination. He looked at it for a few seconds and then glanced at the Countess. "You win," he said to the Count, handing him the amount wagered. The party broke up and everyone returned to their cabins.

Next morning Gerrard noticed a piece of paper that had been slipped under his cabin door. On it was a lipstick mark and the words "Thank you." Explain.

Word search

```
D  I  S  N  A  C  B  F  Y  W  I  E  L  P  B
A  O  I  C  I  Z  A  W  W  K  G  H  Q  A  O
E  D  R  C  L  T  N  E  I  L  C  C  S  W  J
H  Q  E  S  S  A  Y  C  N  E  T  A  L  S  T
D  A  T  A  B  A  S  E  N  T  T  P  T  R  X
F  X  N  H  W  Y  N  S  T  H  I  A  A  S  U
T  O  I  O  R  K  D  D  P  E  B  C  E  B  T
R  B  R  N  E  E  L  L  D  R  K  M  M  P  I
A  D  P  E  U  C  A  J  N  N  F  R  I  S  L
L  O  S  E  G  I  H  D  H  E  H  C  T  J  I
U  N  U  S  R  R  X  T  P  T  O  Z  K  C  T
D  Q  P  E  W  E  O  I  M  N  T  K  E  O  Y
O  I  S  U  P  P  X  U  V  L  C  P  E  B  S
M  W  V  D  U  E  B  V  N  M  O  R  S  O  E
X  F  C  U  L  K  E  X  L  D  I  D  I  L  B
```

ANSI	HEAD	ROM
APACHE	HTML	SEEK TIME
ASCII	HTTP	SERIAL
BIT	ICON	SQL
BPS	JOB	STACK
BSD	LATENCY	THREAD
CLASS	MIPS	TRACK
CLIENT	MODULAR	UNIX
COBOL	NNTP	URL
DATABASE	OS	UTILITY
DNS	PIXEL	VDU
ETHERNET	PRINTER	WAP
FOREGROUND	QUEUE	WORD

Crossword

Across

6. Sob story (6)
7. Pilus (4)
8. Uniform projection (5)
9. Self-respectful (5)
10. Carcajou (9)
12. Row (5)
13. Happy deflection (2-3)
16. Nothing (4)
17. Hispanic (6)

Down

1. Fool (4)
2. Protagonist (4)
3. Tousle (8)
4. Coralled lake (6)
5. Believability (4)
9. Zealot (8)
11. Body of work (6)
12. State of affairs (4)
14. Leave out (4)
15. Pes (4)

26	5	1	8	4	20	17		11	17	4	5	4
20		12		7		1		5		17		20
17	9	18	5	18	17	6		9	7	6	18	17
17		8		17		17		24		12		19
6	7	26	13	16		2	11	8	24	7	25	22
				17		3				8		7
12	15	17	20	6	12		13	12	4	9	12	4
4		23				22		4				
2	26	13	17	20	14	12		2	19	5	20	25
17		5		7		22		17		22		12
20	12	7	9	6		22	8	10	7	5	9	3
15		2		6		17		7		26		8
17	9	3	20	16		3	13	16	2	17	1	21

1	2	3	4 B	5	6	7	8	9	10 Q	11 K	12	13
14	15	16	17	18	19	20	21	22	23	24	25	26

Only two of the shapes below are exactly the same – can you find the matching pair?

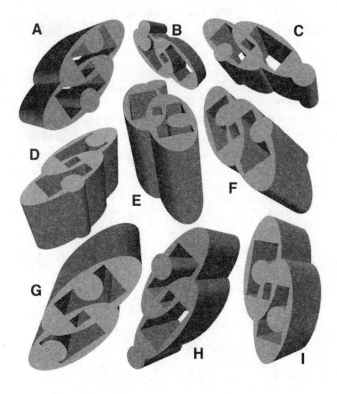

The chapel

Henry Morgan was not a deeply religious man. However, he preferred to play safe and in a crisis he invariably took to prayer. He reasoned that if there was someone who listened, it just might help; if not, no harm was done.

Once again one of his property deals had gone wrong and Henry was in serious trouble. The only thing that could save him from bankruptcy was *force majeure*, an Act of God, such as an earthquake or at least subsidence, as he was heavily insured. For a brief moment he had considered lending a helping hand toward such an event, but the advanced state of forensic science scared him off.

He therefore made his way to his favourite chapel on Mont St. Michel. It was a good hour's walk in the glaring midday sun. On arrival he first sat down to rest his tired legs. When he had finished his prayers a couple of hours later, he found to his exasperation that he was unable to walk back home. He was not incapacitated in any way, nor had anything unusual occurred in the landscape.

Can you explain what had happened?

		5					6	
			1			9		2
9		4				7		
	1		6		7	3		
				1				
			4				8	
	6	9	5				4	
3					9	8		5
	8						9	

The roulette ball is dropped into the wheel at the 0 section. When the ball falls into a number 20 seconds later, it has travelled at an average speed of 3 metres per second clockwise, while the wheel has travelled at an average 2 metres per second in the other direction. The ball starts rolling 50 centimetres away from the wheel's centre. Where does it land? Take pi as having a value of exactly 3.14.

Code grid

6	12	24	17	14	22		12	24	22	9	3	12
12		13		7		24		22		18		18
18	22	25	13	8	24	13		9	18	8	20	3
22		12		15		25		3		18		22
21	17	7	13	15		13	7	12	26	22	15	21
12				16		7				21		23
	4	24	11	13	7	14	3	10	17	22	1	
22		13				18		17				22
6	17	4	4	22	24	8		13	1	24	12	18
5		21		23		8		15		8		14
17	6	8	22	21		20	22	2	12	19	22	11
18		4		12		3		12		24		24
12	4	4	12	15	21		12	7	23	11	20	12

1	2 K	3	4	5	6	7 N	8	9	10	11	12	13
14	15	16	17 U	18	19	20	21	22	23	24	25	26

```
K C E B S N A W I U M E V D J
C O N W Y I W H L A O Y E A V
R R A E E L B B I R V T M V X
A A A A T E R K H T A C L Y H
A A N R L Y S M E U W A T O T
H Y A N A W E Y M P A S K A F
T E D E N G R R T A D N R Z B
X O R P I V N O E M I G G D J
S D O I Y A W A C H E R O N I
U B J P L Y A Z T A S D K E G
X Z M G L F O C O R A I I Y N
O Z O Q D A G C G B K Q F E K
U M J I C O T R A D E C G S Q
O B U U S P V E R P O R O F F
P F R J Y E A E L P O N E R J
```

AA	EDEN	OXUS
ACHERON	EMS	PLATE
AHI	EOD	PO
ALT	GLAN	RENO
ANGARA	HUANG	RIBBLE
AYR	II	ROCK
BRAHMAPUTRA	ILI	ROE
CEDAR	ISHERE	RYE
CONWY	JORDAN	STYX
CREE	NAR	TAW
DON	NEGRO	TOWY
DOVE	NILE	WANSBECK
EARN	OISE	WEY

Masyu

Draw a single continuous line around the grid that passes through all the circles. The line must enter and leave each box in the centre of one of its four sides. Black Circle: Turn left or right in the box, and the line must pass straight through the next and previous boxes. White Circle: Travel straight through the box, and the line must turn in the next and/or previous box.

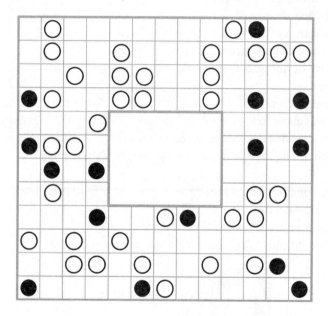

Riddle

The Judgement

A man stood before the judge, charged with killing a long-eared owl, a protected species. Pleading guilty but with extenuating circumstances, the man explained that he had been on a camping trip with his family in a remote region. One day, while they were all swimming in a nearby lake, their camp caught fire and was completely destroyed, leaving them without shelter or food. After going hungry for two days, they came upon the bird, and the man threw a rock that succeeded in killing it. It was cooking and eating the owl, he allowed, that helped them to survive.

The judge, after hearing his story, decided to let the man off. As the man was about to leave the court, the judge called out, "Just as a matter of interest, what does a long-eared owl taste like?" The man paused, thought for a moment and then answered the judge's question.

The judge then called him back. "On second thoughts, I retract my earlier decision," he said. "You will pay a fine of $2,000, and consider yourself lucky I do not send you to prison." What did the man say to cause the judge to reverse his original decision?

Crossword

Across

7. With ice-cream (1, 2, 4)
8. Devoured (3)
9. Overjoy (5)
10. Sniff (5)
11. Mend (4)
12. Shelter (4)
15. Scrub (5)
16. Origins (5)
18. Bishop's seat (3)
19. Rooted (7)

Down

1. Hussy (4)
2. Jumping soldier (11)
3. Spiked spur wheel (5)
4. Curt (5)
5. Bank holding (4-7)
6. Sevensome (6)
11. Stop (6)
13. Take hold (5)
14. Swift (5)
17. Twist (4)

The collision

Henry was a happy man. He had just signed a contract for the supply of 3,000 tons of fertilizer to the Agricultural Cooperative of Maryland. Driving along the busy freeway at some speed in his old Chevrolet, Henry was trying to work out his profit on the deal and toying with the idea of replacing his clapped-out car with a new Cadillac.

He was so absorbed in his thoughts that he was not paying attention to the road. His car veered from its lane, collided with six vehicles in the adjacent lane and overturned. Henry and the driver of one of the other vehicles were killed instantly. The other cars involved in the carnage were complete write-offs. However, no other driver was killed, injured or even scratched. Were they just lucky?

Word search

```
H A S F I E L D H D I S C U S
G O J A R E N A W T N H P R E
R R R R Y B M V W E O O M O N
U D W S E M A G G M L T U A A
N E W Y E L D E M L H P J D L
N R O R T S A E R E T U F W K
I S R L R R H Y E H A T J A L
N T H G I E W O F I T F Z L A
G F T T A S S R E N N U R K W
N O L H T A I B R S E S L S E
F V I I H M C D E Z P A C E C
R A C E L E A D E R D E P K A
E K B L O C K S I E V O K B R
R I D I N G S N M Z L K B O P
U M P I R E T V W O R R A W I
```

ARENA	JOG	RELAY
ARROW	JUMP	RIDING
BIATHLON	LANES	ROADWALK
BLOCKS	MEDAL	RUNNERS
BOW	MEDLEY	RUNNING
DISCUS	ORDERS	SHOTPUT
FIELD	PACE	SPRINT
GAME	PENTATHLON	STICK
GEAR	POLO	THROW
HAMMER	RACELEADER	TRIATHLON
HELMET	RACEWALK	UMPIRE
HORSESHOES	REFEREE	WEIGHT

Sudoku

							7	
		1	8	7	2			3
	7	2				9		
	6			5			4	1
	3		1			8		5
	1							
		5		1			3	
4			6			1		
	2		7	8				4

25	12	17	4	13	7		25	20	14	11	10	24
21		14		18		25		14		7		20
9	10	26	18	24	18	10		13	7	20	12	14
18		14		10		4		10		26		14
12	7	9	18	4		19	18	24	24	21	23	16
13				13		10				15		17
	11	15	17	18	9	22	12	8	21	10	1	
20		7				14		21				14
13	7	3	24	14	18	23		18	9	1	14	5
14		23		2		7		4		14		7
12	19	18	6	14		21	9	19	14	26	25	23
21		1		4		20		18		21		18
12	6	14	15	23	14		26	14	23	20	18	4

1	2 J	3	4	5	6 V	7	8	9	10	11	12 S	13
14	15	16	17	18	19	20	21	22	23	24	25	26

Two-finger salute

This is a difficult one and will require clever questioning. In medieval France, when two opposing forces joined battle it was the custom that the warriors lifted their right arm in a gesture of defiance, forming a "V" with two fingers. This sign was neither meant as abuse nor was it the Victory sign popularized by Winston Churchill during the Second World War.

What then did it signify?

ANSWERS

Answers

Puzzle 2

Puzzle 3

Puzzle 4

5	2	8	1	7	6	9	4	3
4	3	7	8	5	9	2	6	1
1	6	9	2	4	3	5	8	7
2	8	6	3	1	4	7	9	5
7	4	1	6	9	5	3	2	8
9	5	3	7	8	2	4	1	6
6	7	5	9	2	8	1	3	4
3	1	2	4	6	7	8	5	9
8	9	4	5	3	1	6	7	2

Puzzle 5

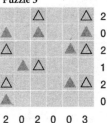

Puzzle 6
Switch horses!

Puzzle 8

3	4	8	9	2	7	1	6	5
5	7	6	3	8	1	9	4	2
9	1	2	6	4	5	3	7	8
6	8	5	1	7	2	4	9	3
4	2	1	5	9	3	7	8	6
7	9	3	4	6	8	2	5	1
1	3	9	7	5	6	8	2	4
8	5	7	2	1	4	6	3	9
2	6	4	8	3	9	5	1	7

Puzzle 9

Puzzle 10

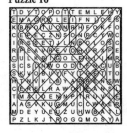

Puzzle 11

Answers

Puzzle 12

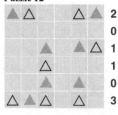

Puzzle 13

Puzzle 14

2	5	7	3	1	8	6	4	9
9	1	8	5	6	4	7	3	2
6	4	3	9	7	2	5	1	8
4	8	1	2	5	9	3	7	6
3	2	9	6	4	7	8	5	1
7	6	5	8	3	1	9	2	4
5	3	2	4	9	6	1	8	7
8	7	6	1	2	3	4	9	5
1	9	4	7	8	5	2	6	3

Puzzle 15

The boy picked a pebble out of the hat and before they had a chance to examine it, dropped it, apparently accidentally, where it was lost among the pebbles on the ground. He then pointed out to the king that the colour of the dropped pebble could be ascertained by checking the colour of the one remaining in the hat.

Puzzle 16

3	4	1	7	2	9	6	8	5
2	9	5	8	1	6	4	3	7
7	8	6	3	5	4	1	9	2
5	3	7	2	6	8	9	4	1
9	1	2	4	3	5	8	7	6
8	6	4	9	7	1	2	5	3
6	2	8	5	4	3	7	1	9
1	5	9	6	8	7	3	2	4
4	7	3	1	9	2	5	6	8

Puzzle 17

Puzzle 18

4	7	6	3	2	5	8	1	9
5	8	9	1	6	4	2	7	3
1	2	3	7	8	9	6	5	4
7	6	8	2	1	3	4	9	5
9	4	1	5	7	8	3	2	6
2	3	5	4	9	6	7	8	1
8	1	4	6	5	7	9	3	2
3	9	2	8	4	1	5	6	7
6	5	7	9	3	2	1	4	8

Puzzle 19

Dave occupied the adjoining room and Pete was being kept awake by Dave's snoring.

Puzzle 20

9	4	1	3	5	2	6	8	7
7	6	2	9	1	8	5	3	4
5	8	3	7	6	4	1	9	2
6	3	9	4	2	7	8	1	5
2	5	4	1	8	3	7	6	9
1	7	8	5	9	6	4	2	3
8	1	5	2	7	9	3	4	6
4	9	6	8	3	5	2	7	1
3	2	7	6	4	1	9	5	8

Puzzle 21

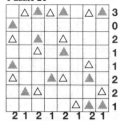

Answers

Puzzle 22

2	6	7	5	1	4	3	9	8
5	8	9	6	3	7	1	4	2
4	3	1	8	9	2	6	5	7
7	1	8	2	6	9	5	3	4
3	2	4	1	8	5	9	7	6
9	5	6	4	7	3	8	2	1
8	7	3	9	4	6	2	1	5
1	4	5	3	2	8	7	6	9
6	9	2	7	5	1	4	8	3

Puzzle 24

8	4	5	9	7	3	1	2	6
1	2	9	8	4	6	3	7	5
6	7	3	1	2	5	4	8	9
5	1	2	3	9	8	7	6	4
4	3	8	2	6	7	5	9	1
7	9	6	4	5	1	8	3	2
3	5	7	6	1	2	9	4	8
9	6	1	7	8	4	2	5	3
2	8	4	5	3	9	6	1	7

Puzzle 25

Puzzle 26

Puzzle 27

3	9	1	4	2	6	7	5	8
7	5	2	9	3	8	4	6	1
4	8	6	7	5	1	9	2	3
8	4	5	6	7	3	1	9	2
9	1	7	5	4	2	8	3	6
6	2	3	8	1	9	5	7	4
5	7	8	3	6	4	2	1	9
1	3	9	2	8	5	6	4	7
2	6	4	1	9	7	3	8	5

Puzzle 28

When Steve fell the first time, the concrete forecourt had only just been laid and was still wet. The soft cement acted as a cushion. By the time the second fall occurred the concrete had set hard, thereby causing multiple fractures.

Puzzle 29

3	9	8	7	4	6	2	1	5
1	4	5	3	8	2	7	9	6
2	6	7	1	5	9	8	3	4
8	2	1	5	6	4	3	7	9
9	7	4	8	2	3	6	5	1
5	3	6	9	1	7	4	8	2
6	5	3	2	7	1	9	4	8
4	8	9	6	3	5	1	2	7
7	1	2	4	9	8	5	6	3

Puzzle 30

Across / Down answers include: ASTRONAUT, SOL, HOT, MOP, MIXED UP, RAF, LET, ALE, FOOL, HAILSTORM.

Puzzle 31

A and G are the pair.

Answers

Puzzle 32

Puzzle 33

Puzzle 34

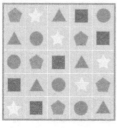

Puzzle 35
4 hamsters and 3 cages.

Puzzle 37

Puzzle 38

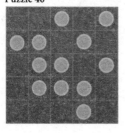

Puzzle 39

3 > 1 < 2	4	5
1 < 4	5	2 < 3
5 > 2	3 > 1	4
2	5 > 4	3	1
4 > 3	1	5	2

Puzzle 40

Puzzle 41

5	7	2	6	8	3	9	1	4
8	6	4	1	7	9	5	2	3
1	9	3	4	5	2	6	7	8
4	1	9	5	3	8	2	6	7
7	8	5	2	9	6	3	4	1
2	3	6	7	4	1	8	5	9
9	2	1	3	6	4	7	8	5
3	4	7	8	2	5	1	9	6
6	5	8	9	1	7	4	3	2

Puzzle 42

Answers

Puzzle 44
C and I are the pair.

Puzzle 45

Puzzle 46

Puzzle 47

Puzzle 48

Puzzle 49

7	3	6	5	9	1	8	2	4
2	4	8	6	7	3	5	9	1
5	9	1	2	4	8	3	7	6
8	6	7	4	3	5	9	1	2
3	1	2	9	8	6	4	5	7
9	5	4	1	2	7	6	3	8
1	7	9	8	5	4	2	6	3
4	2	3	7	6	9	1	8	5
6	8	5	3	1	2	7	4	9

Puzzle 50

1	3	3	4	5	1
4	O	X	X	X	3
2	O	X	O	O	4
3	X	O	O	X	3
4	O	O	X	O	3
1	1	4	3	3	1

Puzzle 51

1	6	2	7	9	3	8	5	4
8	4	5	2	6	1	7	9	3
7	9	3	8	5	4	1	2	6
6	7	8	9	4	5	3	1	2
9	5	1	3	8	2	4	6	7
2	3	4	1	7	6	5	8	9
5	8	6	4	3	9	2	7	1
3	2	7	6	1	8	9	4	5
4	1	9	5	2	7	6	3	8

Puzzle 52

7	6	8	7	6	8	9	8	9	9	8	8
8	7	7	6	7	7	6	6	6	6	6	6
8	8	7	8	8	9	8	9	8	8	9	9
9	7	7	8	8	8	9	7	9	7	8	8
6	6	8	6	7	7	7	8	7	9	7	7
8	9	8	7	8	9	8	9	8	8	7	9
9	8	7	8	9	8	9	6	6	9	8	6
7	8	9	7	6	6	6	8	9	6	6	8
8	6	8	9	8	9	8	9	8	8	9	9
9	9	6	6	9	8	9	8	7	6	7	7
6	7	9	8	6	6	7	8	7	9	8	8
8	9	7	9	8	9	8	9	6	8	9	6

Answers

Puzzle 53

5	3	6	8	7	9	4	1	2
4	9	1	2	3	5	7	6	8
2	7	8	4	6	1	5	9	3
8	4	7	9	1	2	3	5	6
6	2	3	5	4	7	1	8	9
1	5	9	3	8	6	2	7	4
7	6	2	1	9	3	8	4	5
9	8	5	7	2	4	6	3	1
3	1	4	6	5	8	9	2	7

Puzzle 54

The emerald the man was found clutching was a superb replica. He had swallowed the real gem and then emptied the flask of whisky. Before he smashed the crystal dome, he had been faking being inebriated, but after he had drunk the contents of his hip flask, and by the time he was examined in the prison hospital, his blood alcohol level had risen very high.

Puzzle 55

Puzzle 56

Puzzle 57

Puzzle 58

Puzzle 59

Puzzle 61

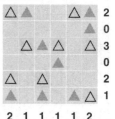

Puzzle 62

Alice had a wealthy boyfriend who wanted to buy her an expensive birthday present. They had shopped together and selected a costly bracelet, but as this would have been difficult for Alice to explain to her husband, she and her boyfriend conspired with the jeweller to go along with the deception and quote George a much lower price.

Puzzle 63

7	9	3	2	8	4	1	6	5
1	8	6	3	5	7	2	4	9
5	2	4	1	9	6	3	7	8
8	6	1	7	2	9	4	5	3
2	4	5	8	3	1	7	9	6
3	7	9	6	4	5	8	2	1
9	1	2	5	7	3	6	8	4
6	5	8	4	1	2	9	3	7
4	3	7	9	6	8	5	1	2

Puzzle 64

Answers

Puzzle 65

Puzzle 66

		P		S	O	M	E	D	A	Y			
		R		E		O		I		F			
S	T	R	I	P	C	L	U	B	S		R		
M		N		O		S		E		O		Q	
A			C	O	N	T	E	R	M	I	N	O	U	S
L		E		D		T		B		T		A	
L		S		C	A	R	B	O	N	S	I	N	K
F	R	E	S	C	O		A		D			T	
O		M		M		P	A	Y	E	E		U	
R	O	B	O	T	I	C		N		X		M	
T		E		N		N		N		O	D	D	L	Y
U	N	D	E	R	G	R	O	U	N	D		E	
N						L		N	S	A	Y		
E	X	E	R	C	I	S	E			S		P	

Puzzle 68

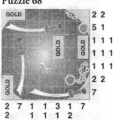

	2	2
	5	1
	1	1	1
	1	1	1
	1	1	1
	2	2
	7

2	7	1	1	3	1	7
2		1	1	1	2
			1

Puzzle 69

K	I	S	S		S	Y	S	T	E	M
N		L		A		P		X	
M	O	T	E		T	H	A	T	C	H
P		U		R		L		
R	E	S	T	A	T	E		R	A	G
R		H		E		F		M	
S	A	G		C	A	R	A	V	A	N
T		D		C		T	
R	I	G	O	U	R		I	B	I	S
V		P		O		A		O	
D	E	L	E	T	E		L	A	N	E

Puzzle 71

2	1	8	6	9	3	7	4	5
4	7	9	1	2	5	8	6	3
6	3	5	4	7	8	9	1	2
8	2	1	9	5	4	3	7	6
7	4	6	2	3	1	5	8	9
9	5	3	8	6	7	1	2	4
3	9	4	7	8	2	6	5	1
1	6	7	5	4	9	2	3	8
5	8	2	3	1	6	4	9	7

Puzzle 72

Puzzle 73

The man was acting as a decoy to draw the policemen away from the club, whose members – some of whom were more than slightly inebriated – drove off in a hurry as soon as the coast was clear.

Puzzle 74

Puzzle 75

2	3	7	8	1	5	6	4	9
9	8	6	2	3	4	1	7	5
1	4	5	6	7	9	3	8	2
7	2	1	3	8	6	9	5	4
4	9	3	5	2	7	8	6	1
6	5	8	4	9	1	2	3	7
3	6	4	9	5	2	7	1	8
8	7	9	1	4	3	5	2	6
5	1	2	7	6	8	4	9	3

Answers

Puzzle 76

Puzzle 77

Puzzle 78

6	5	1	4	7	2	9	8	3
3	2	9	1	6	8	4	5	7
7	8	4	9	5	3	6	1	2
4	6	8	7	2	5	1	3	9
2	9	3	8	4	1	5	7	6
1	7	5	3	9	6	8	2	4
5	4	6	2	1	7	3	9	8
9	3	2	5	8	4	7	6	1
8	1	7	6	3	9	2	4	5

Puzzle 79

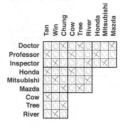

Puzzle 80

Puzzle 81

Puzzle 82

2	4	5	7	9	6	8	3	1
1	8	6	3	5	2	4	7	9
9	3	7	8	4	1	5	2	6
7	5	1	9	3	4	6	8	2
3	9	8	6	2	7	1	4	5
6	2	4	1	8	5	3	9	7
5	6	2	4	7	3	9	1	8
4	1	9	2	6	8	7	5	3
8	7	3	5	1	9	2	6	4

Puzzle 83

Puzzle 84

Puzzle 85

9	7	8	1	5	3	2	4	6
6	2	4	9	7	8	3	5	1
5	1	3	6	4	2	9	7	8
2	3	1	5	6	7	8	9	4
8	9	7	3	1	4	6	2	5
4	5	6	2	8	9	7	1	3
7	8	5	4	2	6	1	3	9
3	4	2	8	9	1	5	6	7
1	6	9	7	3	5	4	8	2

Answers

Puzzle 86

Puzzle 87

Puzzle 88

Puzzle 89

4	3	1	7	9	5	6	2	8
9	2	7	8	4	6	5	3	1
8	5	6	3	1	2	4	7	9
7	4	2	5	6	9	8	1	3
6	1	8	2	3	4	9	5	7
5	9	3	1	7	8	2	4	6
2	7	5	6	8	3	1	9	4
1	6	4	9	2	7	3	8	5
3	8	9	4	5	1	7	6	2

Puzzle 90
E.

Puzzle 92

Puzzle 93

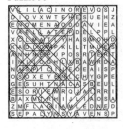

Puzzle 94

Puzzle 96

185

Answers

Puzzle 97
3350 millimetres^2.
Each 20 x 20 square represents 400 mm^2. 1 Square, 10 half-squares, 4 quarter-squares and 11 8th of a squares are used.

Puzzle 98

Puzzle 99
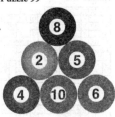

Puzzle 100

Puzzle 101

Puzzle 102
Jonathan had actually lapped the Nigerian runner who, when he crossed the line, still had a lap to go, a fact which Jonathan almost immediately realized.

Puzzle 103

Puzzle 104
The witness was the bank clerk who gave the description of the impostor to the police. By a fortunate coincidence he saw the man and Dawson sitting together in a restaurant the day before the hearing.

Puzzle 105
This is what the note said: "I have a severe case of laryngitis, and on doctor's orders I must not speak as it could be dangerous in my condition. However, I am the manager and if you don't let me go to the front, I will not open the store."

Puzzle 106
(crossword grid)

Puzzle 107
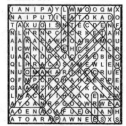

Answers

Puzzle 108

S	W	E	E	T	M	E	A	T			C	O	D	I	F	Y
N		Y									O				O	
A	T	T	E	M	P	T	S				O				R	
R		T		I							O				O	
E	N	F	O	R	C	E	D			V	E	G	A	N		
D		O		K		W				E			G			
R	E	S	T	R	U	C	T	U	R	E	S		R	E	F	E	R
U			H		P		L			N			I			E	
M		C	O	A	C	H		I		G		L		U	
	H	W	E	U	N	U	C	H		D		R	
C	A	C	H	E	T		G		T	I	T	A	N
S		I		A				B		R	
M		L	A	B	O	U	R	S	A	V	I	N	G
I	S	L	E					G		P	

Puzzle 109

8	1	5	4	9	6	7	3	2
7	3	2	1	8	5	4	9	6
6	4	9	2	7	3	8	1	5
5	7	1	3	2	8	6	4	9
4	6	3	9	1	7	2	5	8
2	9	8	5	6	4	3	7	1
9	5	7	6	3	2	1	8	4
1	8	6	7	4	9	5	2	3
3	2	4	8	5	1	9	6	7

Puzzle 110

Puzzle 111

Puzzle 112

Puzzle 113

The six men and John were members of a bomber flight crew during World War II. They had to make an emergency landing on a bare, uninhabited island in the South Pacific, far off any sea lanes. The radio equipment was out of action, and their only hope of being saved was a search operation by the US Air Force or Navy. Weeks passed with ever-smaller rations available to sustain life. When all food reserves were exhausted, they had to choose between dying one by one or cannibalising parts of their bodies. They agreed to start with sacrificing their left forearms. John, being the only surgeon on board, had to be spared to perform the operations. He had to undertake, however, that if they survived he would have his limb amputated within five years after the end of the war. The five-year span was agreed to give John time to learn a different profession. In the event he changed his mind and decided to use the deception, which he hoped would satisfy his former comrades that he had honoured his vow.

Puzzle 114

In fact, Frank Forrester saw an advertisement offering a list of number plates including DEM 10 with N as the year of registration. In other words, the plate read DEM1ON. As this was the somewhat unusual first name of Miller's wife, he knew that Bruce, in his snobbishness, would go for it and pay any price. The new owner was prepared to pay a top market price for the car, but the number plate meant nothing to him.

Puzzle 115

	△				▲	△	**2**
△	▲	▲	▲				**1**
			△		▲		**1**
				△			**1**
						▲	**0**
		△	▲	△		△	**3**
	▲						**0**
	▲	△		▲	△		**2**
1	**0**	**3**	**1**	**1**	**2**	**0**	**2**

Answers

Puzzle 116

Alan Goide suddenly realized that the wrong suitcase had carried his name tag. This proved that the switch was deliberate, probably for the purpose of smuggling drugs.

Puzzle 117

9	4	1	2	8	6	3	7	5
3	6	8	7	4	5	9	1	2
2	5	7	1	3	9	6	8	4
8	2	9	6	1	3	5	4	7
4	7	5	9	2	8	1	3	6
1	3	6	4	5	7	2	9	8
7	8	3	5	6	1	4	2	9
5	1	2	8	9	4	7	6	3
6	9	4	3	7	2	8	5	1

Puzzle 118

Puzzle 119

Puzzle 120

Puzzle 121

7	4	1	3	6	2	9	8	5
2	5	8	9	1	7	3	6	4
3	9	6	4	8	5	2	7	1
9	7	4	8	3	6	5	1	2
8	1	5	2	7	9	4	3	6
6	3	2	5	4	1	7	9	8
4	2	3	1	9	8	6	5	7
1	6	9	7	5	4	8	2	3
5	8	7	6	2	3	1	4	9

Puzzle 122

B and G are the pair.

Puzzle 123

Puzzle 124

Puzzle 125

The hijackers did not take the time to body-search their two victims, so they failed to notice that one had a cellular phone in the front pocket of his jacket. Despite the handcuffs, he managed, with the help of his co-worker, to get hold of the phone and dial 911. Speaking softly, he gave the police the truck's registration number and colour, and by looking out of a small window he was able to describe the route taken by the culprits.

Answers

Puzzle 126

Hexagonal grid values:
1 2 2
3 2 2 2
2 2 2
3 3 3 3
3 3
0 1

Puzzle 127

Puzzle 128

3	5	**6**	7	**9**	8	**4**	2	1
2	4	**7**	3	1	5	9	8	6
8	**9**	1	2	6	**4**	5	**7**	**3**
1	6	4	5	3	**2**	8	**9**	7
7	8	5	9	4	6	**1**	3	2
9	2	**3**	8	7	1	6	5	4
4	3	9	1	**8**	7	2	6	**5**
5	1	**8**	6	2	**3**	7	4	9
6	7	**2**	4	5	9	**3**	1	8

Puzzle 129

¹B	E	²S	E	³T		⁴M	A	⁵P	L	⁶E
A		T		E		L		L		R
⁷S	A	U	C	E	R		⁸S	A	T	E
S		D		T		⁹C		C		C
O		¹⁰C	O	H	E	R	E	N	T	
		¹¹S		T		R		R		¹³O
¹²P	R	E	P	A	R	E	D			O
O		D		L		G		¹⁴S		V
¹⁵S	C	U	D		¹⁶L	O	C	A	L	E
I		C				E		L		R
¹⁷T	H	E	M	E		¹⁸S	P	E	N	T

Puzzle 130

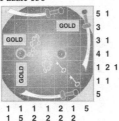

5 1
3
3 1
4 1
1 2 1
1 1
5

1 1 1 1 2 1 5
1 5 2 2 2

Puzzle 131

4
10 2
8 6 5

Puzzle 132

X	A	V	Q	C	O	B	P	Z	J	W	L	E
F	Y	D	I	N	S	H	M	K	T	G	U	R

Puzzle 133

The man was Alexander Fleming, who in 1929 prepared a culture plate of staphylococcus as part of his research programme. The culture was unexpectedly contaminated by spores of *penicillium notatum*. The colonies of staphylococcus disintegrated into a mould. Fleming was sufficiently intrigued to isolate the mould in pure culture. This was found to be a substance which had a powerful destructive effect on many bacteria. The first antibiotic had been discovered.

Puzzle 134

Puzzle 135

9	6	**4**	3	1	7	5	**2**	8
8	**2**	1	6	5	4	3	7	9
3	5	7	8	2	9	1	4	6
2	1	9	5	7	3	**6**	8	4
5	**8**	3	4	9	6	2	1	**7**
7	4	6	**2**	8	1	9	3	5
1	3	8	9	4	5	7	6	2
6	**9**	2	7	3	**8**	4	5	1
4	7	5	1	6	2	8	**9**	3

Answers

Puzzle 136

Norman knew, of course, that the Amazon flows from west to east. It is also obvious that the sky at dawn is lighter in the east, and gradually darker toward the west, while at dusk the reverse is the case. If he had had a watch he would have known instantly, as in the Brazilian winter (summer in the northern hemisphere) the sun rises early in the morning and sets late in the evening.

Puzzle 137

S	I	T	U	P			L	E	A	S	T
H		I		R				R		R	H
R	A	N	G	E	R		M	A	C	E	
U		T		G		G		B			M
G			U	N	D	E	R	L	I	E	
		R		A		N		E			
C	L	E	A	N	S	E	R				S
U		T		T		R		D			T
B	R	I	G		S	O	N	A	T	A	
I		N			U			T			K
C	H	A	L	K		S	U	E	D	E	

Puzzle 138

'Harry Winston will be at the function and he knows an imitation if he sees one, so I had better take the real necklace from the bank vault.'

Puzzle 139

D	I	S	K		S	P	E	C	I	E
E		H		A		I		I		V
B	A	R		C	A	N	T	A	T	A
		E		C		F		O		C
C	O	N	G	E	N	E	R			U
A		E		L		A		L		E
R			T	E	S	T	C	A	S	E
D		R		R	H		M			
I	S	O	L	A	T	E		B	O	B
A		L		T				D		S
C	L	E	V	E	R		B	A	K	E

Puzzle 140

5	7	4	1	8	9	3	6	2
6	2	9	5	7	3	1	4	8
3	8	1	6	4	2	7	5	9
7	5	3	2	1	8	4	9	6
9	6	8	4	5	7	2	1	3
1	4	2	9	3	6	8	7	5
2	9	7	3	6	4	5	8	1
8	3	5	7	9	1	6	2	4
4	1	6	8	2	5	9	3	7

Puzzle 141

Rudolf's friend had decided to bungee jump from the top of Nelson's Column and had asked for the height so that he could arrange the correct length of elastic cord. Rudolf's miscalculation meant that his friend's rope was too long, thereby causing his death.

Puzzle 142

The Countess's necklace was in fact genuine and given to her by her rich lover. The Count had been told that the necklace was a well-made paste piece, which the Countess had bought herself. Gerrard knew that the piece was genuine but, seeing the expression on the face of the Countess, he guessed the situation and gallantly lied and paid the Count.

Puzzle 143

Puzzle 144

T		H		D			L		C
W	E	E	P	I	E		H	A	I	R
I		R		S			G		E
T	O	O	T	H		P	R	O	U	D
		E			A		O		
	W	O	L	V	E	R	I	N	E
		E			E	T			
S	C	U	L	L		I	N	F	O
I		V			S		M		O
Z	E	R	O		L	A	T	I	N	O
E		E			N		T		T

Puzzle 145

C	A	L	I	B	R	E		K	E	B	A	B
R	O	U		L			A	E		R		
E	N	G	A	G	E	D		N	U	D	G	E
E		I		E		J		O		W		
D	U	C	H	Y		S	K	I	J	U	M	P
		E		T		I			I		U	
O	V	E	R	D	O		H	O	B	N	O	B
B		X			P		B					
S	C	H	E	R	Z	O		S	W	A	R	M
E		A		U		P		E	P		O	
R	O	U	N	D		P	I	Q	U	A	N	T
V		S		D		E		U		C		I
E	N	T	R	Y		T	H	Y	S	E	L	F

L¹	S²	T³	B⁴	A⁵	D⁶	U⁷	I⁸	N⁹	Q¹⁰	K¹¹	O¹²	H¹³
Z¹⁴	V¹⁵	Y¹⁶	E¹⁷	G¹⁸	W¹⁹	R²⁰	F²¹	P²²	X²³	J²⁴	M²⁵	C²⁶

Puzzle 146

C and H are the pair.

Puzzle 147

Mont St. Michel in Normandy, France, is a tidal island, cut off from the mainland at certain high tides. Henry had forgotten to enquire when the next one was due before setting out on his pilgrimage.

Puzzle 148

1	3	5	9	7	2	4	6	8
8	7	6	1	4	5	9	3	2
9	2	4	8	3	6	7	5	1
4	1	8	6	5	7	3	2	9
6	9	3	2	1	8	5	7	4
2	5	7	4	9	3	1	8	6
7	6	9	5	8	1	2	4	3
3	4	2	7	6	9	8	1	5
5	8	1	3	2	4	6	9	7

Puzzle 149

In the 9 space. The ball travels at a speed of 5 metres per second (relative to the wheel) for 20 seconds, making a distance of 10,000cm in a clockwise direction. The circumference of the wheel is 320 (well, 319.96!) centimetres (2 x pi (3.14) x radius (50 .95cm)). The ball must then travel 31.25 laps of the wheel (10,000 divided by 320 = 31.25), placing it one quarter of the way around the wheel in a clockwise direction, in the 9 space.

Puzzle 150

B	E	L	U	G	A		E	L	A	P	S	E
E		I		N		L		A		R		R
R	A	V	I	O	L	I		P	R	O	M	S
A		E		C		V		S		R		A
T	U	N	I	C		I	N	E	X	A	C	T
E			H		N				T		Z	
	F	L	Y	I	N	G	S	Q	U	A	D	
A		I		R		U				A		
B	U	F	F	A	L	O		I	D	L	E	R
J		T		Z		C		O		C		O
U	B	O	A	T		M	A	K	E	W	A	Y
R		F		E		S		E		L		L
E	F	F	E	C	T		E	N	Z	Y	M	E

D	K	S	F	J	B	N	O	P	V	Y	E
G	C	H	U	R	W	M	T	A	Z	L	V	X

Puzzle 151

Puzzle 152

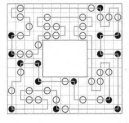

Puzzle 153

When the judge asked what long-eared owl tasted like, the man had replied, "The taste of the owl was a cross between a golden condor and a bald eagle." (Both are protected species.)

Puzzle 154

¹J		²P		³R	⁴T		⁵S		S
⁷A	L	A	M	O	D	E		⁸A	T	E
D		R		W		R		F		P
⁹E	L	A	T	E		¹⁰S	C	E	N	T
	T		L		E		D		E
¹¹D	A	R	N			¹²T	E	N	T
E		O		¹⁴B		P
¹⁵S	C	O	U	R		¹⁶R	O	O	T	¹⁷S
I		P		A		I		S		K
¹⁸S	E	E		¹⁹S	E	S	S	I	L	E
T		R		P		K		T		W

Answers

Puzzle 155

There were only two vehicles involved in the collision. The vehicle which collided with Henry's was a transporter truck carrying a load of five cars.

Puzzle 156

Puzzle 157

6	5	8	9	3	1	4	7	2
9	4	1	8	7	2	6	5	3
3	7	2	5	4	6	9	1	8
8	6	9	2	5	7	3	4	1
2	3	7	1	9	4	8	6	5
5	1	4	3	6	8	7	2	9
7	8	5	4	1	9	2	3	6
4	9	3	6	2	5	1	8	7
1	2	6	7	8	3	5	9	4

Puzzle 158

P	S	Y	C	H	O		P	R	E	F	A	B
U		E		I		P		E		O		R
N	A	M	I	B	I	A		H	O	R	S	E
I		E		A		C		A		M		E
S	O	N	I	C		K	I	B	B	U	T	Z
H				H		A				L		Y
	F	L	Y	I	N	G	S	Q	U	A	D	
R		O				E		U				E
H	O	W	B	E	I	T		I	N	D	E	X
E		T		J		O		C		E		O
S	K	I	V	E		U	N	K	E	M	P	T
U		D		C		R		I		U		I
S	V	E	L	T	E		M	E	T	R	I	C

D	J	W	C	X	V	O	Q	N	A	F	S	H
E	L	Z	Y	I	K	R	U	G	T	B	P	M

Puzzle 159

The men holding up two fingers were archers and they were indicating that the fingers used to pull back the bowstrings were intact. (It was common practice in medieval times for prisoners of war to have their first two fingers cut off by their captors.)